ADVISORY COUNCIL FOR THE MISUSE OF DRUGS

Members

Mr Vivian Ahman

Mrs Joy Barlow

Reverend Martin Blakeborough

Mr Raj Boyjoonauth

Mr Alexander Cameron

Dr William Clee

Dr Michael Donmall

Dr Anthony Duxbury

Professor Griffith Edwards

Ms Vivienne Evans

Dr Laurence Gruer

Ms Kim Hager

Mr Paul Hayes

Mr Russell Hayton

Ms Lorraine Hewitt

Mr Peter Housden

Mr Roger Howard

Mr Alan Hunter

Professor Ronald Jones

Professor Malcolm Lader

Professor Otto Meth-Cohn

Mr Michael Narayn Singh

Dr Diana Patterson

Mr Colin Phillips

Sir Michael Rawlins (chair)

Ms Kay Roberts

Mrs Patricia Roberts

Dr Roy Robertson

Dr Sue Ruben

Mr Ian Sherwood

Professor John Strang

Mr Peter Walker

Mrs Barbara Whiteley

deaths

A Report by The Advisory Council on the Misuse of Drugs

London: The Stationery Office

ISBN 0 11 341239 8

Printed in the United Kingdom for The Stationery Office
TJ001134 C30 5/00

CONTENTS

Chapter	*Page*
Preface	xi
Summary and recommendations	xii
1. The purpose and scope of the report	1
Introduction	1
The substances which the report covers	2
What is a drug-related death?	3
Structure of the report	3
The intended readership	4
A report with very practical intentions	5
2. Toxicology and Pathology of immediate deaths related to drug misuse	7
Introduction	7
Immediate death following drug misuse	7
The substances which will be considered	7
The need to consider the different possible mechanisms of death	7
A framework	9
Major toxic effects	9
Lungs and breathing	9
Heart	9
Strokes	10
Liver	10
Kidney	10
Infective complications	11
Fatalities due to accident or violence	11
Factors which will influence the risk associated with drug use	11
Mode of use	11
Drug purity	12
The role of contaminants	12
The significance of dependence and tolerance	12
Substances	14
Heroine (Diamorphine)	14
Methadone	15

Other Opioids   15
Cannabis   15
Cocaine   16
Ecstasy   17
Benzodiazepines   18
Alcohol as cause of death   18
Other drugs   19
Amphetamine sulphate   19
Lysergic acid diethylamide   19
Volatile substances   19
Multiple substances   19
Conclusions   20

3. **Social, Situational, and personal factors which may contribute to
   risk of death associated with drug misuse**   21
   Introduction   21
   User characteristics   22
   Gender   22
   Age   23
   Employment, income and social class   23
   Mental health status, depression and suicide   24
   Location   25
   Homelessness   25
   Drug availability   26
   Risk perception and risk response amongst drug users   26
   Conclusions   28

4. **The present system for collecting data on drug deaths and problems
   with them**   29
   The approach which we take   29
   The current system and its problems: England and Wales   30
   Doctors notify the coroner   33
   The coroner   33
   Post mortem toxicological examinations   35
   The Registrar of Births and Deaths   36
   Office for National Statistics   36
   The current system and its problems: Scotland   38
   The current system and its problems: Northern Ireland   39

Variations in procedures across the constituent parts of
the UK: some general comments 39
Other sources of information on drug-related deaths in the UK 40
Home Office: Statistical Bulletin of Notified Addicts 40
St George's Hospital Medical School: National Programme on Substance
Abuse Deaths 40
Department of Environment, Transport and the Regions 40
Communicable Disease Surveillance Centre (CDSC) 41
International data 42
Data system on drug misuse: conclusion 42

5. **Improving the Data Base** 45
The problem 45
Making improvements 45
Data on deaths due to virus-related chronic illness 46
The responsibility of coroners 47
The coroner and use of forensic toxicological examinations 47
Recording of relevant information by the coroner 48
Scotland and the role of the Procurator Fiscal 49
The role of ONS in strengthening the data collection 49
Data on drug misuse deaths and road traffic accidents 50
International comparisons 50
Improving the data base: conclusions 50

6. **Drug-related deaths: Some key output from the presently available
data sources** 51
Looking for the most meaningful categorisation 51
Acute drug-related mortality in England and Wales based on the
EMCDDA definition 52
Age and "accidental" deaths due to drug misuse 55
Years of life lost 56
Drug-related mortality by geographical location 56
Drug-related mortality by social deprivation 57
Deaths by drug type 58
Drug-related deaths in Scotland 58
Drug-related deaths in Northern Ireland 59
Conclusions 59

7. **Methadone**   61

Introduction   61

Methadone: mode of use and therapeutic benefits   62

Pharmacology and toxicology   62

Factors influencing prevalence of methadone-related deaths   63

Increased prevalence of methadone prescribing   63

Methadone and interaction with alcohol and other drugs   63

Deaths by accidental poisoning   64

Methadone: optimising clinical usefulness while reducing the risks of overdose   64

The very strong need to prevent methadone diversion   64

Recommendations relating to the prescribing of methadone   64

The strong need to monitor and curtail methadone-related deaths   66

The Scottish experience with methadone   66

The need for research on alternatives to methadone   67

Conclusion   67

8. **Reducing deaths from the immediate effects of taking drugs**   69

Introduction   69

Prevention of immediate deaths with a focus on the drugs   70

The drugs of prime concern   70

Loss of tolerance as an underlying danger   71

Preventing injected drug misuse as a salient issue   71

The need for stricter controls over prescribing   72

The problem in general   72

Benzodiazepines   72

Volatile substance abuse (VSA) as a continuing problem   73

Advice on Ecstasy   73

Prevention of immediate deaths and the role of particular agencies   74

The crucial role of drug services   74

The need for policies on risk assessment   74

Risk assessment should be followed by implementation of an action plan   75

The responsibility to prevent diversion of prescribed drugs   76

Drug services, mental health and suicide prevention   76

Prevention of drug-related deaths and the role of primary care   77

Accident and Emergency Departments   78

Emergency services, their response to overdoses, and the response of people
who witness the overdose   78

Penal and enforcement services   81

Police arrestees   81

Prisons and aftercare 82
Preventing deaths from traffic accidents and violence 83
Road traffic accidents 83
Homicides 83
Conclusions 84

9. **Reducing deaths from chronic illnesses** 85
Taking the problem seriously 85
The extent of the problem 85
The viruses 86
HIV 87
Prevention of HIV infection 87
Hepatitis C 89
Hepatitis B 91
Other types of infection which may be transmitted by or associated with drug misuse 92
Drug misuse and virus infections: cross-cutting elements in strengthening the helping agency responses 92
Prisons and the prevention of virus infections 93
Conclusion 94

10. **Priorities for a policy framework** 95
The need for a policy framework 95
Improvement in the data system and its operational use at national and local level 96
A better informed public awareness of the problem set by drug-related deaths 96
Awareness to embrace both acute drug-related deaths and those resulting from chronic illnesses 97
A heightened level of knowledge and commitment and an attitudinal shift across all relevant agencies 97
Multiple improvement in relevant practices across agencies and audit of performance 97
Agency practices to be aimed strongly and persistently at reduction in injected drug use 97
An end to lax and irresponsible prescribing and a radical curtailment of methadone-related deaths 98
A strengthened response to drug misuse by the Prison Service 98
Better liaison between agencies 98
Enhanced investment in professional training 99

The need to target social deprivation   99
Attempts are needed actively to involve drug users themselves in responsibility
for reducing drug-related deaths   99
A more determined attempt to reach drug users who are outside agency contact   99
Response to the needs of families   100
A crucial role for DATs and DAATs   100
Better investment in research which can help prevent drug-related deaths   100
Causes for optimism   100

Appendix A   Prevention Working Group   103
Appendix B   Acknowledgements   104
Appendix C   Coroner's Certificate After Inquest   105
Appendix D   References   107

Index   117

PREFACE

1. The Advisory Council on the Misuse of Drugs (ACMD) is a body constituted under the Misuse of Drugs Act 1971. As preface to this ACMD report, we offer a brief note on the why and how of its being written.

2. As to the question of <u>why</u>, the report is written in discharge of ACMD's statutory responsibility to advise ministers. Although that, strictly, is the totality of ACMD's target responsibility, it has also traditionally sought to address the extraordinarily wide range of people at many different front lines who between them make any intended policies into working realities.

3. Over its 28 years of existence ACMD has previously produced reports of that kind which have both advised ministers and made recommendations which have sought to be useful to the wider field.

4. In selecting any particular topic as focus for attention, ACMD will pick on questions which it not only deems to be important and topical, but where in its judgement a review is likely to result in a set of down-to-earth and achievable recommendations on how some facet of drug use can be dealt with better. That is exactly the perspective within which ACMD decided in November 1997 that it was appropriate to direct its resources to a report on prevention of drug-related deaths. In 1999, reducing drug-related deaths became a target within the National Drugs Strategy.

5. Regarding the <u>how</u> of the exercise which then followed in support of that aim, ACMD deputed the preparation of this report to its Prevention Working Group (PWG). PWG is a multi-disciplinary group made up of ACMD members and of people who have been co-opted for the duration of a particular task. Government officials attend and the work is facilitated by a secretariat. The production of the report involved PWG members in 17 full day meetings, the hearing of 14 invited witnesses, review of 5 specially commissioned background papers, examination of a good deal of published research, and the commissioning of a piece of research of its own. A draft report was presented to a full meeting of the Council in November 1999, and the finalised text was sent to Ministers in December 1999.

6. It is that text which is now published. In our judgement, the prevention of drug-related deaths is not just topical but a matter of pressing urgency. The number of such deaths should, can and must be substantially reduced, and we believe that the advice given in this report should help achieve that goal.

SUMMARY AND RECOMMENDATIONS

Chapter 1   Purpose and scope of the report

1.1   In England and Wales something between 1076 and 2997 deaths of drug misusers occurred in 1998 as a result of overdose. Some of those deaths were suicides but most were accidents. That we give such wide margins is unsatisfactory but reflects the current problems with the database. The trend is in any case upwards.

1.2   Rates of drug-related deaths appear to be no less in Scotland. In Northern Ireland the numbers remain low.

1.3–1.4   These figures take no account of deaths due to virus infections, to motor vehicle accidents, or to incidental violence. Under these headings also, the data are far from complete. Within the foreseeable future deaths due to virus diseases transmitted by drug injection may exceed those from overdose and other immediate effects of drug misuse.

1.5–1.6   A caring society must be expected to expend effort in preventing premature deaths from all and any causes. Within that perspective, preventing deaths from drug misuse warrants due attention. Such deaths are today a cause for concern in Britain, in several other European countries, in North America and in Australia.

1.7–1.8   Reduction of drug-related deaths is identified as a performance indicator within the National Plan of the United Kingdom's Anti-Drugs Co-ordinator. It should be feasible to reduce significantly the death rate among drug users while continuing to work by every means possible to prevent misuse itself. There is no contradiction between these two intentions.

1.9   A blind eye has over recent years too often been turned to the fact that drug misuse is a life-threatening condition. Changed attitudes are therefore needed as well as multiple actions.

1.10–1.11   A major focus of this report will be on preventing deaths from the misuse of controlled drugs. We will also deal with volatile substance abuse (VSA). Drug interactions are important and we will at times be looking at the interactions between illicit drugs and alcohol.

1.12   In our view it would be remiss not to acknowledge that smoking kills about 120,000 people each year, and between 28,000 and 33,000 people die annually as a result of alcohol.

1.13–1.14   In this report we will distinguish between immediate deaths, due largely to overdose, and delayed deaths which may occur as a result of complications resulting from HIV, hepatitis B (HBV) or hepatitis C (HCV), possibly many years after the initial virus infection.

1.15 The structure of the report is outlined and a brief synopsis given of each chapter.

1.16 ACMD has a primary responsibility to advise Ministers. The report is also intended to be useful to people who deal with drug problems at many different front lines.

1.17 The report seeks to offer an analysis of a complex problem and has within it an element of review. The aim, however, is not to conduct analysis for any abstract sake, but to provide a statement which can serve as a catalyst for strong and multiple actions. We are calling for a new, integrated, and determined initiative on the prevention of deaths due to drug misuse. We want to see in place a planned and coherent national effort. Small fragmented efforts cannot meet the need.

Chapter 2 Pathology and Toxicology of immediate deaths related to drug misuse.

2.1–2.2 This is a review chapter. It identifies the mechanisms involved in causation of immediate or near-immediate deaths from illicit drugs, or from interactions between those drugs and alcohol.

2.3 Among the factors determining whether an individual succumbs to the toxicity of a particular substance, the actual properties of the substance, together with the amount used, rank very highly.

2.4–2.6 We start by looking at the problem in terms of what body systems can be affected, and by describing the effect of drugs on breathing. The commonest way in which drugs cause immediate deaths is through their effect on respiration.

2.7–2.8 The next system to be considered is the heart and circulation. Reduction of the heart's output can result from a number of different effects of drugs.

2.9–2.10 The misuse of certain drugs can result in stroke.

2.11–2.12 The liver is another organ which can in some instances be affected, and kidney failure also can follow drug misuse.

2.13 Injected drug misuse can result in septicaemia and infection of the heart valves, besides transmission of the virus infections which are the focus of Chapter 9.

2.14–2.15   Going on from the impact of drugs on body systems, we discuss the relationship between drug use and deaths due to accident or violence. Suicide is commonly associated with drug misuse.

2.16–2.17   We turn then to consideration of some factors which may influence the degree of risk associated with any particular type or occasion of drug use. Injection of drugs carries particularly high risks of many kinds.

2.18–2.19   Another risk factor can be the purity of the drug. The contaminants with which drugs have been diluted or cut, may on occasion have contributed to risk but this factor has tended to be exaggerated.

2.20–2.23   Marked tolerance to brain effects can occur with heroin use or with other opioids. Withdrawal, with its associated loss of tolerance, can put the opioid drug user at very considerable risk if they then again take a drug, without awareness that their previous tolerance has been reduced.

2.24–2.25   We then consider the risks of overdose which may attach to particular drugs, starting with heroin. We outline the possible mechanisms for heroin-related deaths.

2.26–2.27   Methadone is another opioid which today, in the UK, is a frequent cause of drug-related deaths but we postpone detailed discussion of this issue until Chapter 7. We identify some other opioids which from time to time become available on the illicit drug scene. We note the dangers which may be associated with injection of ground-up tablets of Diconal, or the injection of other opioid drugs which are available in tablet form.

2.28   There are no reports of acute death directly related to toxicity from cannabis. There is increasing evidence that cannabis may be associated with road traffic accidents. The extent to which the association speaks to causation, is undetermined.

2.29–2.32   Cocaine can cause sudden death through a variety of mechanisms. Chronic cocaine use can increase the likelihood of a person sustaining a bleed from a pre-existing brain aneurysm. A cocaine overdose can result in greatly elevated body temperature and can cause an agitated delirium which may have fatal consequences.

2.33–2.34   Ecstasy (MDMA) and similar drugs are now popular in the UK as "dance drugs". A few deaths occur each year due to disorders of the heart rhythm, overheating, liver damage, or bleeds into the brain. A further complication which may occur occasionally with Ecstasy, is death due to water intoxication. This can result from mistaken interpretation of messages urging Ecstasy users to drink fluids so as to avoid dehydration when dancing in a hot environment.

2.35–2.36   Benzodiazepines are much safer drugs than the barbiturates which they largely replaced in medical practice. The dependence potential of benzodiazepines should not, however, be ignored. In the UK benzodiazepines have today become widespread drugs of misuse. They contribute to drug-related deaths through fatal respiratory depression, particularly so when these drugs are taken together with opioids or alcohol.

2.37–2.38   In our listing of specific drugs we also consider alcohol. Alcohol can kill young people in a number of different ways and these are detailed. It is a mistake to think that, either among young or older people, alcohol only causes death by chronic disease.

2.39   We give briefer attention to some other drugs. Amphetamine sulphate has potential to cause toxicity of kinds similar to cocaine, but at present in the UK is making only a small contribution to the count of drug-related deaths.

2.40   LSD does not cause toxic deaths but there are anecdotal reports of it causing death by accident when the user is intoxicated, and does something unguarded in a deluded or hallucinated state.

2.41   We make brief mention in this chapter of volatile substances (a topic on which ACMD reported previously in 1995). Deaths fell from a peak of 151 in 1990 to 58 in 1996 but are now showing a slight upward trend.

2.42–2.45   Having looked at the dangers of different drugs separately, we enter a strong reminder that many drug-related deaths are caused by interaction between several different drugs taken at, or around, the same time. Every drug combination that occurs in the course of drug misuse adds to the dangers, is unpredictable in its consequences, and may all too easily lead to tragedy. And we again stress that alcohol often makes a contribution to these interactions.

2.46   We believe that the science we have laid out in this chapter can provide valuable insights which will inform the needed prevention strategies which we outline later. Beyond the direct and practical implications of this science for those kinds of actions, we would also suggest that a reading end to end of the facts given here, may serve as corrective to any idea that drugs are no more than symbols, fun or recreational substances. Drugs can kill suddenly and unexpectedly. They can do so in many different and interacting ways which can overwhelm many different body systems.

Chapter 3   Social, situational and personal factors which may contribute to risk of death associated with drug misuse

3.1   The previous chapter dealt with the dangers of drugs within a toxicological perspective. The present chapter analyses drug use as an individual behaviour which occurs in a social context. Social, situational and personal risk factors may exacerbate the risk of drug-related death.

3.2–3.5   The history of social science research on this topic is briefly traced. Promising work is underway but there is still a shortage of relevant studies.

3.6–3.7   The first factor which we examine is that of gender. Considerably more men than women die from drug misuse. However, if correction is made for the actual numbers of males and females who are injecting and rates calculated against these base numbers, that conclusion may at times be weakened or even reversed.

3.8–3.9   Age is another factor which we consider. Different studies give somewhat different results but the median age for death among injecting drug users is generally in the late twenties or early thirties. With increasing duration of use all sorts of adverse life experiences may impinge on the user and increase the risk of drug-related death. It is not only naïve users who are at risk.

3.10–3.11   Drug deaths tend to be more common amongst unemployed and unskilled workers. There is strong evidence of a relationship between social deprivation and risk of drug-related death. But the relationships between social disadvantage and drug misuse do not run only one way. Drug misuse is itself likely to exert a negative influence on social adjustment.

3.12–3.13   Poor mental health and particularly depression, are likely to add to the risk of suicide among drug users. HIV and AIDS may also exacerbate such risk.

3.14–3.15   Most drug-related deaths occur in some kind of residence. The injection of drugs in public places may be a risk factor because the drug is likely to be injected quickly and without caution.

3.16   The availability of any drug may be expected to bear on the prevalence of its use, and the risk of death. One aspect of availability is price.

3.17–3.19   The drug injector's life is permeated by risk of many kinds, but they frequently underestimate the risk they are taking. Behaviours which to the observer appear "risky" may be viewed in a different light by drug users themselves.

3.20–3.21   Many drug deaths occur in the company of other users but frequently there is delay between overdose, and seeking help. Some research has recently been focusing on those strategies which drug users may use on their own initiative, so as to decrease risk of overdose.

3.22–3.23   We conclude that further and better understanding of matters which we have discussed in this chapter is likely to be of considerable help to prevention. Although drugs are a prime cause of drug-related deaths, the totality of the personal and social context needs to be taken into the reckoning. Prevention of drug-related deaths must deal with the drugs. But it must also be sensitive to other and wider issues which may bear on, and diminish or exacerbate, the inherent riskiness of the drug.

Chapter 4   The present system for collecting data on drug-related deaths.

4.1   This and the following two chapters are closely related. Here we describe the data system operating in different countries within the UK, and identify the problems within it. Chapter 5 makes suggestions for improvement in this system. Chapter 6 presents some key outputs from the presently available sources.

4.2   To have in place a system which can provide trustworthy data on drug-related deaths is of fundamental importance to the national drugs strategy, and to the initiative on prevention of drug-related deaths which we are proposing in this report.

4.3   We do not, however, believe that these deaths can provide a surrogate indicator for drug-misuse prevalence. It is possible to envisage drug-related deaths going up while the problems of drug misuse went down within the general population in particular, and *vice versa.*

4.4   As an essential first step we have attempted to develop detailed understanding of how the present system works.

4.5   The intention of the system should be to capture all deaths where the stated substances are in some degree implicated in the individual's death, while at the same time excluding all deaths which are not relevant.

4.6   As mentioned at the outset, the major focus of this report is on illicit drugs but we would expect volatile substance abuse (VSA) deaths also to be captured. Alcohol is not our primary concern but its interactions with illicit drugs are of such importance that there is a case for trying to get alcohol-related deaths within the same general reporting frame as we will be proposing.

4.7   We identify the major underlying types of "relatedness" in substance-related deaths as :deaths due to acute poisoning or acute illness; due to chronic illness; due to road traffic accidents; due to a poisoning by some other party.

4.8   We then turn to a detailed description of the current system in England and Wales. In Table 4.1 a summary is given of the problems we see as lying within this sector.

4.9–4.11   The first step in compiling these statistical data is when doctors notify the coroner. A surprising problem is that there are coroners working in high drug prevalence areas who will never certify death as related to drug misuse.

4.12–4.13   The coroner generally orders a post mortem to be carried out by a pathologist, and the coroner or coroner's officer may collect additional information on the deceased.

4.14   Following the post mortem, the coroner may hold an inquest. In the case of a drug-related death there is a choice of six mutually exclusive verdicts: Dependence on drugs; Non-dependent abuse of drugs; Accident/ misadventure; Suicide; Open; Homicide.

4.15   We do not think a coroner can be expected to differentiate between those first two categories. Furthermore, these two categories are not mutually exclusive as against the other categories. That framework is, in our view, inadequate for purposes of systematic data collection.

4.16–4.17   Following the inquest, the coroner certifies the death in Form 99 which we have reproduced as Appendix 1. The headings of that form are described.

4.18   Where more than one substance is recorded by the coroner, there is generally no indication which substance was most responsible for the death. There is no indication given as to route of drug administration, nor of whether a toxicological examination was carried out.

4.19   It is in our view unsatisfactory that the recording of important matters is, in effect, being left here to a voluntary and unstructured annotation on a report form, rather than being collected in a formal, systematic manner.

4.20   The coroner may or may not require a toxicological examination to be undertaken, and we could not discover the criteria on which this decision is made.

4.21   When the coroner has reached a verdict and completed the certificate, the next step is for that certificate to be sent to the Registrar of Births and Deaths. The Registrar does not receive the reports made by the pathologist, nor those made by the police.

4.22 ONS (Office for National Statistics) appears at present to have no routine way of checking back with the coroner's office, if information is incomplete.

4.23–4.24 On the information supplied, the relevant officer at ONS codes up causes of death within terms of the ninth revision of ICD (International Classification of Diseases). There are five available codes reflecting the structure outlined in 4.14. We see the current ONS coding structure as logically unsatisfactory for much the same reasons as pertain to the framework employed by the coroner (4.15).

4.25–4.27 Further complications arise from the way in which the five main three-digit ICD9 codes are sub-divided into more specific four-digit codes. The four-digit codes cover a range of legal and illegal substances including such entries as "arsenic and its compounds". The current ONS approach is therefore likely to be considerably over-inclusive. We thus have a system here which is likely to be both over- and under- inclusive, with a very uncertain balance of outcome.

4.28–4.29 The current approach cannot reveal whether a stated drug was primarily responsible for a death. Tabulations by specific drugs are thus of uncertain interpretability.

4.30 ICD10 will be adopted by the various national statistical officers at different dates in 2000 or 2001.

4.31 We turn next to the system which is operating in Scotland. There, all suspicious deaths must be referred to the procurator fiscal instead of to a coroner, and the cause of death is determined by a pathologist.

4.32–4.34 In 1994 the General Register Office (GRO) in Scotland put in place new arrangements for collecting information on drug-related deaths. Among other things, the role of forensic pathologists was clarified. These arrangements have led to improved data quality.

4.35 A brief note is given on the data collection system operating in Northern Ireland. It is similar to that in England and Wales.

4.36 We express concern about the variation in procedures operating across the constituent parts of the UK. For problems of very common cross-country public health concern, it seems to us disadvantageous if data collection systems are allowed to vary in their definitions.

4.37 Having examined the various central national systems we look at certain other sources of information on drug-related deaths.

4.38–4.40 The Department of Addictive Behaviour at St. George's Hospital Medical School, London has a project which invites coroners and procurators fiscal,

to provide on a voluntary basis more detailed data than are given on routine forms. We commend this initiative but do not think that it can substitute for formal revision in the official processes.

4.41–4.43   The Department of the Environment, Transport and the Regions (DETR), has recently conducted a project which gives information on the presence of drugs in road traffic accident casualties. The results showed a considerable increase in the proportion of fatalities with the presence of a drug compared with a similar study in 1985-87, although the most common drug found, cannabis, can remain in the body long after any effect.

4.44–4.47   The Communicable Disease Surveillance Centre (CDSC) has some data on virus diseases where drug infection is likely to be making a contribution to transmission, but other than in relation to HIV the picture is very incomplete.

4.48–4.49   Initiatives have been mounted to determine comparative rates of drug-related deaths in different European countries. Variations between countries in their data collection systems at present make interpretation difficult.

4.50   We conclude that the current system for collecting and reporting on drug-related deaths in the UK stands in need of considerable amendment and strengthening. There is valuable experience on which to build, but the fact remains that at present the system for generating data on drug-related deaths in Britain cannot provide information of the quality needed.

Chapter 5   Improving the data base

5.1–5.2   What is apparent from Chapter 4 is the lack of reliability in the available data on drug-related deaths. For informed and effective policy formulation in this area, better underpinning with good quality data is a mandatory requirement.

5.3–5.5   We go on to identify point by point what we see as needing to be done. It seems to us better to build on the present system rather than sweep it away and start again.

5.6   Any improvements in the data system are likely in the short term to distort the interpretation of trends.

5.7–5.9   Improvements in data on deaths due to virus illnesses are an important part of the requirement. *We recommend that a national reporting and surveillance system similar to that currently focusing on HIV deaths, should be put in place for HBV (hepatitis B virus) and HCV (hepatitis C virus). We also recommend that repeat national sample surveys on the virus status of clients attending drug treatment agencies be conducted on a two-yearly basis.*

5.10   We then turn to recommendations bearing on the future responsibilities of coroners. *We strongly recommend that the Coroners' Society of England and Wales should be consulted on the feasibility and acceptability of any proposals which will impact on their work.*

5.11   We are worried about the inconsistent way in which post mortem toxicological examination is being used by coroners in England and Wales although we suspect that the situation is better in Scotland.

5.12–5.13 The very large number of cases being considered by coroners each year does however deserve to be noted, and any future proposals on toxicology should be made with awareness of this fact. Mandatory toxicological testing might slow the work requirements of this office in an unwelcome way.

5.14   However, we *strongly recommend that toxicological screening should always be ordered by the coroner in England and Wales where he or she has reason to believe that controlled drugs are implicated, and we suggest some criteria which might determine this decision.*

5.15–5.16 *We make a strong recommendation that the choice of verdicts available to the coroner in relation to the sort of case with which we are concerned should in future be limited to four rather than six categories. The two overtly drug-related categories should be eliminated leaving as choices: accident/misadventure; suicide; open; homicide. Questions relating to drugs would then be treated separately. We therefore suggest revision in part 5 of the coroner's certificate, with a series of specific questions on the possible involvement of drugs in any death. These questions should in future be given answers in every relevant instance.*

5.17   The primary role of coroners is of course simply that of determining cause of death, and that should be acknowledged. But we do not believe an objection that collection of the kind of data we now propose is outside the coroner's remit, can carry conviction. In certain instances coroners already collect data of a kind which takes them beyond their strictly defined responsibilities, so there is precedent for what we are now asking.

5.18–5.19 We would not want to see the coroner's at present unstructured recordings squeezed out by the proposed new structured enquiries outlined in 5.15–5.16. *We do not believe that our suggestions will have large resource implications but we recommend that any extra support needed by coroners should be met.*

5.20   *We see the Coroners' Society as having a vital role in providing further training on the role of its members in relation to the recording of the type of information on the involvement of drugs information which we are proposing, and we recommend that resources should be found to support a training initiative.*

5.21   *We recommend that the same revisions in recording format be applied by procurators fiscal in Scotland and coroners in Northern Ireland.*

5.22   The proposals we make in relation to the role of the coroner and procurator fiscal will allow ONS to collect more detailed and reliable date on drug-related deaths, and are of fundamental importance to improvement in the data system.

5.23   *The questions which arise around how the ICD coding frame is best to be revised are complex. We recommend that a short life technical working group should be brought together to reach agreement on a consistent coding framework to be used in future across England, Wales, Scotland, and Northern Ireland.*

5.24   *We recommend that ONS should establish a formal way of checking back, when needed, with the coroners office.*

5.25   *We would like to encourage further research on the relationship between drug misuse and road traffic accident fatalities.*

5.26   *Work on international comparisons of drug-related mortality rates deserves further support.*

5.27   We conclude that there are a number of evident and feasible separate ways in which data collection on drug-related deaths can be improved. We would however again stress that the aim must be to get a total system working better. *We strongly recommend that the necessary consultations to help set up a new overall system for collection of high quality data on drug-related deaths are quickly got under way, with the needed resources to support the establishment of the system then duly found. The country's response to the problem set by deaths due to drug misuse will be grossly handicapped until the recommendations made here are met.*

Chapter 6   Drug-related deaths: Some key outputs from the presently available data sources.

6.1   We outline the three different available approaches to categorisation of drug-related deaths. The EMCDDA (European Monitoring Centre for Drugs and Drug Addiction), is most restrictive. What we refer to as "ONS restricted" is intermediate in this regard, while the standard ONS approach is least restrictive and the one most likely to be over-inclusive.

6.2–6.3   In Figure 6.1 and Table 6.1, we present data derived using the EMCDDA definition on drug-related deaths in England and Wales, 1979-1998, for males and females separately. Within this approach the number of deaths in 1998 came to 1076. The restricted ONS approach gives a total of 2250 while the standard ONS approach puts the figure at 2922. But there can be no doubt that in England and Wales from about 1980 onwards, deaths related to drugs misuse have increased very significantly for men, and significantly but less steeply for women.

6.4   Using that ONS restricted approach, we present in Figure 6.2 data for England and Wales on male drug-related deaths, 1979-1997, broken down by age group. For the greater part of the period it was the age group 20-29 which was most at risk.

6.5–6.6   Using the restricted approach, ONS calculates that for the year 1995 drug-related deaths accounted for 5% of total male years of life lost, a figure approaching that due to road traffic accidents. We caution that the classificatory approach employed here probably inflates the number of drug-related deaths although other factors may at the same time be causing some underestimates.

6.7   Techniques are now available to ONS which should allow pinpointing of death rates to particular residential areas, down to the level of different housing estates.

6.8–6.9   There is a strong positive relationship in England and Wales between social deprivation and rates of drug-related mortality, so much so that for men aged 15-44 deaths among the most deprived group are six times the rate observed among the least deprived. There is a similar relationship between deprivation and drug-related deaths for women although here the relationship is not so strong.

6.10   The involvement of different drugs in reported fatalities is examined, and year on year it is heroin misuse which is making the largest contribution.

6.11–6.13   The statistics suggest that in Scotland the previous upward trend in drug-related deaths has at least for the time being, somewhat levelled out. Heroin is again the drug of predominant importance. Mentions of methadone have decreased over the last four years, while benzodiazepines are of increasing importance.

6.14–6.16   We conclude that the data which we are able to present in this chapter fall far short of constituting the kind of reliable and comprehensive picture of trends and situations which is needed. It is not a happy state of affairs that on such a core statistic as annual number of deaths due to drug misuse, estimates vary threefold according to the approach used. Despite these difficulties some reasonably confident conclusions can be drawn from the data presently available and these conclusions are summarised. The existing data can provide a limited characterisation of certain aspects of the present situation. More persuasively they point to trends.

Chapter 7   Methadone

7.1   In England and Wales there were in 1995 estimated to be about 30,000 people receiving methadone maintenance treatment for their opioid dependence. Deaths in which methadone is mentioned have increased over recent years, and have become a cause for concern. We question whether, even now, that concern has become sharp enough.

7.2   This chapter provides advice on how the prescription of methadone to drug users should be handled in ways which will increase benefit, and decrease associated risks. *Within an overall initiative to reduce drug-related deaths, we recommend that action to prevent methadone-related deaths must be a priority component.*

7.3   The problems of methadone-related deaths has also become a worrying problem in some other countries.

7.4–7.5   We outline the therapeutic uses to which methadone can be put in the treatment of opioid dependency. There is strong and multiple evidence in the research literature to support the contention that methadone, when given in adequate dosage and with adequate supervision, is likely to produce tangible benefit of several kinds. One of these benefits is reduced risk of death.

7.6   At present in the UK any medical practitioner can prescribe methadone for treatment of opioid dependence and there is minimal central regulation. *Training and supervision in this kind of treatment need to be strengthened.*

7.7   Wide variation can exist between individuals in the way in which the drug is accumulated or cleared within the body. Methadone has a fairly narrow window of clinical safety.

7.8–7.12   We review factors which may influence the prevalence of methadone-related deaths. Such factors include the background fact of a recent increased prevalence of methadone prescribing. The risks of interactions between methadone and alcohol and other drugs, are stressed. Deaths occasionally occur due to accidental poisoning of a child who has had access to prescribed drugs, and *we recommend that when methadone is dispensed clear warnings should be given on the bottle.*

7.13   The question which needs to be addressed is how to maximise the benefits while decreasing the risks of methadone-related deaths.

7.14   If too restrictive and inflexible controls were put in place on the therapeutic use of methadone, the untoward consequence might be that more individuals would continue longer with their highly dangerous intravenous use of illicit drugs.

7.15   With that point conceded, we believe that over recent years the agency approach to prescribing and dispensing of methadone has often been too lax. Diversion of methadone is a serious problem, and most deaths from this drug involve overdoses occurring in people who have got hold of diverted supplies. *Methadone prescribing should in future be conducted in a way which puts more emphasis on preventing diversion and commensurate measures should be instituted.*

7.16   We fully support the recommendations on methadone prescribing made in the recently revised Department of Health guidelines, and we make some compatible suggestions. The remedies will involve new training, new commitment and new institutional safeguards, and repeat review. *In particular we recommend that the normal practice for methadone should be for methadone to be taken under daily supervision for at least six months and often longer.*

7.17   There are inalienable responsibilities which lie with the individual prescribing doctor to give all medicines responsibly. *Health authorities should monitor the quality and adequacy of prescribing of methadone in their geographical areas.*

7.18   *With due safeguards in place, the further extension of methadone availability is likely to save lives and is a development we recommend.*

7.19   We wish to emphasise that in our view the current national level of methadone- related deaths is entirely unacceptable. *We recommend that deaths from methadone should be monitored locally by DATs. National monitoring by ONS should allow feedback to the local level. Nationally we recommend that reduction by an agreed percentage in these deaths should be a performance indicator, but we are aware that improved data collection may for the time being distort the picture.*

7.20   We present data on recent Scottish experience with methadone which demonstrate persuasively that when proper safeguards are in place, including a high level of supervised consumption, increased prescribing of methadone can be accompanied by decrease rather than increase in methadone-related deaths. We see the Scottish experience as strongly supporting our contention that the safety of methadone maintenance treatment, for the individual and the community, will be determined by the care with which the treatment is delivered.

7.21   *We recommend that as a matter of urgency that Department of Health plan trials on alternative therapeutic agents to methadone in the treatment of opioid addiction.*

7.22   Patients as well as doctors, pharmacists and agency workers, need to be more aware of the dangers which can result from methadone and there is a need for much keener awareness at institutional levels. *We recommend that active steps are taken to ensure such awareness, and see DATs as taking a leading role.*

Chapter 8   Reducing deaths from the immediate effects of taking drugs.

8.1–8.2   We distinguish between deaths which occur as immediate or near immediate consequences of drug misuse (the focus of this chapter), and deaths due to chronic disease resulting from virus infections transmitted by injecting (Chapter 9). Some of the recommendations made in the present chapter will also bear on the concerns of the following chapter.

8.3   Preventing drug misuse must in the long term be the best way to prevent drug-related deaths, but ahead of that achievement much can be done to reduce the level of premature death among drug misusers.

8.4–8.7   We identify the drugs which are currently of most major concern as causes of immediate drug-related deaths. Heroin and methadone deaths constitute the prime but not the exclusive problem. We put up a warning signal about cocaine, see benzodiazepines as making a contribution to the problem, and note that VSA continues to kill young people in significant numbers.

8.8   Loss of tolerance is a factor frequently implicated in fatalities. *We recommend that prisoners on release from gaol and clients who have been detoxified or who are completing residential care, are given warning against this danger.*

8.9   Injection of a drug constitutes an especially dangerous route of use. *We recommend that drug treatment services should review their policies to ensure that clients who are not injecting are encouraged never so to do, while those who are injecting are encouraged to cease the practice. We believe that the calmly, rationally but repeatedly stated message 'Don't inject, injecting is too dangerous" should become part of treatment agency culture. We recommend that DATs should make sure that staff training is available on treatment methods which will help avoidance and cessation of injecting.*

8.10   Account has, however, to be taken of the fact that many drug users are not in current contact with a treatment agency, and the "injecting is too dangerous" message must be carried to this wider population. *We recommend that the HEA, in England, the corresponding body in Wales, and HEBS (Scotland) should conduct public information campaigns to carry the needed message widely and ensure that it is sustained.*

8.11–8.13   It is unacceptable that a small number of doctors through poor prescribing practice are contributing causally to addict deaths, and *we commend a licensing scheme for doctors which ties in with their level of expertise.* Prescribing to addicts of controlled drugs in tablet form or in ampoules is in general highly inadvisable. *We recommend that persistent irresponsible prescribing to drug misusers should not be tolerated, and means to prevent such behaviour should be strictly enforced. We would recommend that such cases be referred to the GMC.*

8.14–8.15   We turn then to the problem set by the prescribing of benzodiazepines to drug misusers and stress that these drugs are both dangerous and easily diverted. *We recommend that every prescribing agency should have a policy which will so far as possible avoid prescribing these drugs to new patients and which will assist current patients to come off them, GPs also should tighten their practice.*

8.16   *Special attention should be paid to the dangers which can arise from combined use of opioids, benzodiazepines, and alcohol. We recommend that agencies should warn against such behaviour, and this message should also be given as part of public health advice.*

8.17–8.18   We give a brief note on prevention of VSA deaths, a topic which was the focus of a recent ACMD report. *We recommend that continued attention to this problem is needed.*

8.19–8.20   A brief note is also given on prevention of Ecstasy deaths, another topic on which ACMD has recently given advice.

8.21–8.22   We then examine, sequentially, the role of some particular agencies in prevention of immediate drug-related deaths, starting with the crucial role of specialist drug agencies. *We recommend that every such agency should develop and put in place explicit policies for the prevention of immediate drug-related deaths (and also of course for deaths from blood borne virus diseases, as will be discussed in the following chapter). DATs should assist and monitor the implementation of these policies.*

8.23–8.27   Within those policies *we recommend that with the support of DATs procedures for risk assessment should be developed, and a person-specific action plan implemented to reduce the risk of drug-related death. We make suggestions on the possible contents of these approaches. We recommend that the training implications should be met.* Agencies must avoid entering into a complicit relationship with clients which inhibits everyone concerned from trying to reduce the risk of premature death.

8.28   On occasion, overdose may occur on the premises of a drug agency. *We recommend that staff should be trained in resuscitation techniques and naloxone kept on site.*

8.29   *Drug agencies should be aware of their responsibility to prevent diversion, and we recommend that training should support this ethic. We recommend that staff should also encourage their clients to take responsibility to avoid behaving in a way which may increase risks to their own lives, or to those of other people.*

8.30–8.34   Still focussing on the responsibility of specialist services, we turn to mental health needs and suicide prevention. *We recommend that drug agencies and mental health services should strengthen their abilities to deal with misusers who are experiencing mental health problems.* In our view this has up to now been a sector of service need which has not received sufficient attention. *We recommend the development of closer liaison between the different providers, and enhanced training.*

8.35–8.38   Within our review of the specific responsibilities of different parts of the care system, we focus next on the highly important issue of the role of primary care in the prevention of drug-related deaths. We identify specific interventions available to the GP and other primary care workers. Action continues to be needed to increase the competence in this type of work among all those concerned. *We recommend that DATs should support and monitor the capacity of primary care workers to assist in the prevention of drug-related deaths.*

8.39–8.41   Here we look at the important role of A and E departments in preventing immediate deaths from drug misuse. *We recommend that information should be handed out to all presenting drug misusers, giving relevant health advice. DATs should help establish such practice. Hospitals should satisfy themselves that arrangements for resuscitation of people who have overdosed are satisfactory.*

8.42   We then consider the situation which may develop around the immediate event of overdose, what may be done by the person who witnesses an overdose, and the role of the emergency services which may be called. *We recommend that a call to a person who has overdosed should be viewed as a medical emergency, confidentiality should be maintained, and DATs should help formalise these expectations locally.*

8.43   Relatives and friends who are likely to be witnesses to an overdose should be given guidance on what to do. *This is something we would expect agencies which are in contact with drug users to accomplish.*

8.44–8.45   We believe that ambulance staff should satisfy themselves that arrangements for dealing with this kind of emergency are satisfactory. *We recommend that naloxone should be made available to paramedics and that they are trained in its use.*

8.46–8.49   *We also recommend that the proposal that drug users or their relatives are issued with naloxone is subject to a carefully designed pilot project.*

8.50   We discuss the role of forensic medical examiners(police surgeons)and suggest that their contact with an arrestee should where appropriate be encouraged.

8.51   A high proportion of people who are arrested by the police are drug takers. *We recommend that police surgeons should, where appropriate, speak to the arrestee about referral to help, and information should be available in the police station.* We commend the development of the Drug Arrest Referral Scheme. Arrestees have sometimes died in police custody following cocaine induced delirium. *We recommend that police forces are given guidance on how to identify and deal with this problem.*

8.52–8.55   ACMD has previously issued a number of reports on the care of drug users who are imprisoned and on their after care. We see prisons as potentially having a positive role in preventing drug-related deaths. We commend the recently established CARAT scheme, but are disappointed by the disorganisation which up to now seems too often to have affected the penal response to drug misusers. *In our view it is crucial to prevention of drug-related deaths that the after-care of drug using prisoners should be identified, community liaisons established, and individualised care plans put in place. There should be opportunity for methadone maintenance to be continued while a drug user is in prison.*

8.56   We are concerned about the lack of current information on the role of drug use in contributing to road traffic deaths. *We recommend that drug agencies should be more active in bringing to the attention of their clients the risk which may attach to drugged driving.*

8.57   Drugs may in some instances contribute to disinhibited and dangerous behaviour. Agencies should be aware of these risks.

8.58   We thus conclude that across and between agencies there is a wide spectrum of measures which are feasible, and which should be put in place so as to reduce fatalities among drug users which are caused by the immediate effects of drugs. An intensive, broad and sustained initiative of the kind we propose would, in our view, be likely to save a very considerable number of lives.

Chapter 9   Reducing deaths from chronic illness

9.1-9.2   Awareness of the threat posed to injecting drug users by illnesses resulting from hepatitis infections is at present far too poorly developed. At the outset of this chapter we state fairly and squarely our belief that *hepatitis among drug misusers should now be seen as cause for intense public concern, and for major attention within the overall initiative on prevention of drug-related deaths which this report proposes. HIV deserves continuing attention. But the prevention of hepatitis must no longer be seen as a minor side-show to action on HIV. The sense of energy and concern which earlier characterised the response to HIV needs to be captured in a new and broader initiative on prevention of injection-transmitted virus diseases.*

9.3   It is regrettable that the country is encountering an immensely threatening public health problem without the data with which to monitor population trends and the effectiveness of policies.

9.4–9.7   We describe characteristics of the different types of virus which may be transmitted by injecting. Only 5% of adults infected with hepatitis B will develop long term viral infection, but as many as 80% of those exposed to hepatitis C may carry the virus long-term.

9.8   The only data currently available on deaths from virus related causes due to earlier drug injecting, are for HIV. By the end of 1998 there had in Scotland been 279 deaths of injecting drug users due to AIDS. We believe that Britain has over recent years achieved very considerable success with prevention of HIV, but the fact that at first drug agency contact even a few clients are still found to be HIV positive suggests that there is no room for unguardedness.

9.9–9.12   We consider, in turn, the prevention policies which are required in relation to different virus infections. We start by briefly revisiting HIV, the subject of three previous reports by Council. This country has over recent years achieved an important measure of success in curtailing the rates of HIV occurring among injecting drug users. Policies to reduce the spread of HIV are bound to have some impact on other relevant virus diseases, and vice versa. An important development since Council last reported on AIDS is the availability of more effective drug treatments. There must, however, be concern over development of strains of the virus resistant to treatment.

9.13–9.18   In England and Wales, among long term injectors a recent study found that 62% were HCV positive and 52% HCB positive. In the UK, estimates for the number of former and present injectors infected with HCV range between 152,000 and 228,000. Recent data from the USA suggest that

1.8% of the general population have hepatitis C infection, with injecting drug use the main agent of dissemination.

As regards policies needed for prevention of hepatitis C, of central importance is the highly infectious nature of this virus as transmitted by blood-to- blood contact. In Chapter 8, we have already said that it is essential that non-injectors are encouraged never to inject. Given the infectivity of hepatitis C this message is of the very greatest relevance if transmission of HCV is to be curtailed. In line with advice given in Chapter 8, we wish here again to emphasise the need to get addicts who are already injecting help to move them away from their injecting.

9.19   The hepatitis C virus is more robust than the HIV virus, and we give advice on decontamination of injecting equipment.

9.20   Transmission of hepatitis C between sexual partners is uncommon. *The use of condoms should however be encouraged as a sensible preventive measure if one partner is HCV positive.*

9.21–9.23   A combination of Interferon and Ribavirin in the long term will result in the loss of the hepatitis C virus from the blood in 40% to 50% of those treated. *In that earlier treatment will give better results, we recommend enhancement of opportunities for voluntary testing for HCV.*

9.24–9.25   About 15% – 20% of injectors who become hepatitis B carriers will be at risk of later developing cirrhosis or liver cancer. *Early testing of virus status is again of great importance. Partners of injecting drug users will also need to be tested, in that HBV is rather easily transmitted sexually.*

9.26–9.27   Unlike with hepatitis C, a vaccine to protect against hepatitis B is available, and at low cost.. *We recommend that vaccination against this virus should become part of the childhood vaccination programme in the general population. Meanwhile and until that policy is in place, we recommend that it is good practice to offer immunisation to all injecting drug misusers.*

9.28   Hepatitis D only occurs in people infected with hepatitis B, so vaccination against HBV will protect against hepatitis D also.

9.29   *Specialist advice on the treatment of hepatitis B and hepatitis C infected users should be sought from a hepatologist, and this should be routine agency practice.*

9.30   Drug injectors are at risk of developing septicaemia and helping agencies should be aware of the need to liaise with physical medicine.

9.31–9.33   Having discussed prevention in relation to different viruses as considered individually, we go on to look at cross cutting elements needed to strengthen the response of helping agencies as a whole. *We identify a need for enhanced staff training if the problem set by blood borne viruses is to be more effectively tackled. More use of routine testing for HCV with associated counselling, strong and consistent health messages to drug users on the dangers of injecting and sharing, and the continued provision of clean injecting equipment to all injectors must all be on the agenda. Strengthened liaison with specialist medical services is needed. We are aware that the provision of sterile water has cost implications, but in the face of the HCV epidemic we must now strongly recommend this step provided it is only made available in single dose ampoules so as to avoid the danger of cross infection. Besides these specifics we call for a broad change in agency awareness so as to make prevention of chronic virus related illnesses and associated deaths an ongoing priority part of such agencies' work. The energy which was previously directed at curtailing HIV must now be broadened into action directed at the totality of the relevant blood borne virus diseases.* We do not go so far as to make recommendations on all possible items of paraphernalia but believe that this issue needs to be kept under review.

9.34–9.38   We consider the role of prisons in the prevention of virus infections among drug users. We recommend continually updated education programmes to inform staff and prisoners on the relevant risks. We recommend initiatives which will make decontaminants widely available, coupled with instructions on their use. We recommend that hepatitis B vaccination should be made available to all people entering prisons, with uptake of this advice duly monitored.

9.39   At worst there is a worrying symmetry between the injectors' belief that virus infections "can't happen to me" and with their dealing with the injecting habit postponed until too late, and public belief that preventing the public health problem set by drug-related virus transmission can be postponed. *Action across the whole range of injection transmitted virus diseases is now urgently required, and should not be postponed.*

Chapter 10   Priorities for a policy framework

10.1–10.4   In this chapter we make suggestions as to how the diverse actions which are needed for the prevention of drug-related deaths and which are identified in this report can be given cohesion within an overall policy framework which will support the initiative for which we are calling. We set out a total of 16 explicit elements which will contribute to the building of that framework.

10.5   *Firstly, improvement is urgently needed in the data system and its operational use at national and local level. An effective policy initiative cannot operate blind to the facts.*

10.6–10.7   *An essential element which will contribute to the building of a strong and integrated policy response must be a better informed public awareness of the problems set by drug-related deaths. The public need to know how important this issue has become for the nation's health both in terms of overdose fatalities and the danger of viral transmission. We highlight the role of the media.*

10.8–10.10   *We call for a heightened level of knowledge and commitment, and an attitudinal shift across all relevant agencies. Multiple improvement is needed in the relevant practices across agencies, and with audit of all relevant performance.We emphasise the importance of agency practices being aimed strongly and persistently at reduction in injected drug use, as a vital element within the initiative which this report is proposing. Never inject, injection is too dangerous.*

10.11   *We call for an end to lax and irresponsible prescribing and a radical curtailment of methadone-related deaths. Deaths due to methadone have become a cause for national reproach. It is deeply unsatisfactory that energy and resources are aimed in one sector of activity at reduction in drug-related deaths, while practices are allowed to continue elsewhere which flagrantly risk increase in deaths.*

10.12   *A considerably strengthened response to drug misuse by the Prison Service is required, and we hope that previous inertia will now be overcome.*

10.13   *We make a recommendation for enhanced investment in many relevant aspects of professional training. An educational and training initiative must be intrinsic to the success of the overall policy initiative.*

10.14   *The need for better liaison between different types of agency has become apparent as several points in this report, and we see this as a strong general theme within an overall initiative.*

10.15   *There is a need for continued and strengthened action directed at the amelioration of social deprivation. Deprivation can breed social conditions which encourage the more dangerous forms of drug misuse, and which thus enhance the risks of drug-related death.*

10.16   *Attempts are needed to involve drug users themselves in responsibility for reducing drug-related deaths. We recommend that a message should be given that drug users have a personal responsibility to avoid overdose and virus infection, and that they should not risk the lives of their partners or friends. Users themselves need to be brought into partnership with the policy effort, rather than their being treated only as 'the problem', and as having no hand in the solution.*

10.17   *A more determined attempt is needed to reach drug users who are outside agency contact. To concentrate only on the role of drug agencies in the prevention of drug-related deaths while many people who are outside agency contact are at risk of overdose or of contracting a virus infection, is truly ostrich-like.*

10.18   *Responses to the needs of the families of drug users should in several ways be strengthened. We believe that families can contribute to prevention of drug-related deaths and they may need help when a tragedy has occurred.*

10.19   *We define the role of DATs as crucial to the successful implementation of everything we are proposing.*

10.20   *The final, and sixteenth factor which we see as necessary to the successful implementation of the overall initiative which we propose, is investment in the kind of research which can help prevent drug-related deaths. This area can provide a test-bed for how the research and policy connection in the broader drugs arena can be better handled.*

10.21–10.22   *In conclusion, we want to express a view based on objective consideration of the problems, identification of the many opportunities which are susceptible to action, and our sense of the strengths of what is now a very experienced field. That unequivocal view is that the incidence of drug-related deaths in this country can, will and must, in the near future be substantially reduced.*

1 THE PURPOSE AND SCOPE OF THE REPORT

Deaths due to drug misuse in this country are currently at the highest level ever recorded and rising. The problem lies not only with overdoses and other acute causes of death but also with fatal long-term consequences of HIV and hepatitis. We outline the contents of a report which identifies a range of actions to reduce these deaths.

INTRODUCTION

1.1 Official statistics suggest that there were more than 2300 drug-related deaths identified in England and Wales in 1998 due to accidental or intentional overdose, and with a rising trend. While this will account for only a small proportion of all deaths (around 0.6% for men and 0.2% for women), because of the young age at which they occur they approach the number of years of working life lost through road traffic accident fatalities (78,000 years of working life were lost due to road traffic accidents in 1997. ONS figures) Another way to put the matter in perspective is to state that a young person who is injecting heroin has about a 14 times higher risk of death than someone who is not.

1.2 Rates of drug-related deaths appear to be no less in Scotland [paragraphs 5.10–5.11]. In Northern Ireland the numbers remain low [para 5.12].

1.3 However, the position is worse than those official statistics suggest. These take no account of drug-related deaths from HIV/AIDS (of which there were about 40 in 1997), nor other blood borne virus diseases such as hepatitis B and C, nor motor vehicle accidents.

1.4 The fact that there may be between 152,000 and 228,000 present or former injecting drug users in the UK infected with hepatitis C, is a cause for concern because of the premature deaths which will occur from cirrhosis and cancer of the liver over the next 10-30 years. The numbers who die prematurely from these causes – maybe 30% – seem likely greatly to exceed those who will die from overdose and the other immediate effects of drug misuse.

1.5 Society expends a good deal of effort in preventing premature deaths from all causes. That is a characteristic of a caring and civilised society, and should apply no less to drug misusers than it does to other classes of people. The previous paragraphs amply demonstrate why preventing deaths from drug misuse warrants attention as a subject in its own right.

1.6   As we have been deliberating on this report we have been surprised at the large volume of material which is available on the subject of drug-related deaths. Australia, which has in recent years proved a research powerhouse on drugs issues, has, for example, produced studies on trends in opiate overdose deaths in Australia and, nearer home, work has been undertaken in the UK and in other European countries. The material is not only concerned with the number of deaths but also deals, for example, with information about the ways in which drugs cause death and the likely circumstances of death, and the interventions which may reduce the numbers.

1.7   The National Plan of the United Kingdom's Anti-Drugs Co-ordinator which was published in April 1999, includes among its performance indicators one to reduce the number of drug-related deaths.

1.8   Some people might want to argue that all available resources should be directed at prevention of drug misuse, with prevention of deaths then taken in passing. ACMD attaches considerable importance to the primary prevention of misuse but is also committed to supporting harm minimisation, whenever and wherever opportunities for reducing any aspect of drug-related harm can be identified. Within that perspective we believe that it should be feasible significantly to reduce the death rate among drug users, while continuing to work by every means possible to prevent misuse. We believe that even if for the time being misuse remained at a high level, related deaths can and should be significantly reduced. It is not necessary to wait on the day.

1.9   As well as seeking to identify a range of particular opportunities for action on prevention of drug-related deaths, we believe that there is a necessity, also, to work for a heightened awareness of the urgent national, local, and across-agency responsibility to meet the problem with determination. Stridency would be unhelpful, but we believe that it is appropriate to state that, in our view, a blind eye has over recent years too often been turned to the fact that drug misuse is a life-threatening condition. Changed attitudes will be needed as context for the strengthened and multiple actions.

THE SUBSTANCES WHICH THE REPORT COVERS

1.10   The terms of reference of the Advisory Council naturally point this report towards preventing deaths from the misuse of controlled drugs. However we have in the past felt it to be within the bounds of our responsibilities to report on volatile substance abuse (VSA), and noted within our last report a statistical relationship between deprivation and VSA deaths. We will touch again on that subject later in this report.

1.11   We will also be mindful that often drugs are not misused in isolation but are taken in combination with one another. Their interaction in the body may render them more likely to cause death than if they were each taken alone. Alcohol, given its widespread consumption, will often be one of the substances in the combination.

1.12   While this report must necessarily confine its scope, we feel that it would be remiss not to acknowledge that premature deaths also occur from using other substances. We are aware that smoking kills about 120,000 people each year ('Smoking Kills' White paper published by Department of Health 1998), while alcohol is responsible for between 28,000–33,000 deaths annually (information given by Alcohol Concern). Premature deaths from drug misuse are part of a wider phenomenon. But that does not mitigate the responsibility to do everything possible to reduce deaths from illicit drugs and VSA.

WHAT IS A DRUG-RELATED DEATH?

1.13   Immediate, or virtually immediate deaths, may arise directly from the pharmacological action of the drug. They may occur as the result of a "normal" dose, an accidental overdose or deliberate overdose (suicide) by the user. Less directly the drug may cause the taker to lose their normal judgement or control, leading to an accident. Less directly still, the taking of drugs may lead to violent behaviour which causes death of others; to the deaths of children through accidental overdose of a drug which has fallen into their hands; and to accidents, notably in road vehicles, killing third parties. Drugs can even contribute towards death without their being taken, when violent rivalry occurs between dealers.

1.14   Immediate deaths from drug misuse need to be distinguished from delayed deaths which arise from virus infections such as HIV and hepatitis viruses, which can be transmitted through injecting. The conditions may not lead to death for many years after initial infection.

STRUCTURE OF THE REPORT

1.15   Following this introductory chapter the report is structured in the following way:–

Chapter 2 This reviews what is known about the **toxicology and pathology of immediate deaths related to drug misuse**. In cross-cutting fashion it looks at how various different systems within the human body may be impaired or overwhelmed by the action of drugs, and then goes on to look at the dangers associated with particular drugs. Drug interactions are also discussed.

Chapter 3 Drugs are important as constituting the obvious ultimate agent of a drug-related death. But in reality the causes of a death are usually multiple, complex and interactive. Building on the previous chapter, Chapter 3 therefore goes on to consider the **social, situational, and personal factors which may contribute to risks of death associated with drug misuse**.

Chapter 4 For purposes of policy, official data need to be grouped so as to give the best possible estimate of how many deaths are being caused by drug misuse in any one year. **Here we describe the current system for gathering data on drug-related deaths, identifying some problems within it.**

Chapter 5 **Makes suggestions for improvements in the data gathering system which will strengthen the reliability of the output.**

Chapter 6 This gives a synopsis of **the most recent data on the numbers of drug-related deaths in the UK.** We examine the relationship between such mortality and age, sex, and social deprivation. An estimate is also offered of the number of years of life lost due to drug-related deaths.

Chapter 7 The most widely used drug in the treatment of opioid dependence is **methadone**. A serious public health problem has arisen over recent years because this useful drug can, if laxly prescribed, itself cause fatalities. We make recommendations on how such dangers may be reduced.

Chapter 8 This chapter makes a series of recommendations on strategies for **reducing deaths from the immediate effects of taking drugs**. Here the larger part of the problem concerns death by accidental overdose among injecting drug users, but deaths by suicidal overdose also make a contribution.

Chapter 9 This addresses the parallel question of the need to identify **strategies for reducing death from chronic diseases resulting from drug misuse.** We argue that the importance of preventing deaths from acute causes should not be allowed to overwhelm the fact that deaths from virus infections (HIV and hepatitis B and C), are likely in the medium or long term to build up to become a very significant or even the major element within the totality of drug deaths.

Chapter 10 In this final statement we seek to bring together thinking from the previous chapters, and outline what we see as **priorities for a policy framework**.

THE INTENDED READERSHIP

1.16   In the preface we stated our hope that in addition to this report meeting our responsibility to advise Ministers, it would be useful to people who deal with drug problems "at many different front lines". An attempt to spell out the nature of those front lines may be useful in conveying a sense of the breadth of action which will be needed if drug-related deaths are to be effectively tackled. The following list does not imply an ordering in terms of importance or priority and it is undoubtedly incomplete:

Administrators in central and local Government; Accident and Emergency departments; ambulance staff and paramedics; Drug Dependence Units and community drug teams; NHS Managers; NHS Commissioners; obstetric departments and midwives; voluntary sector drug agencies of many different types and needle exchanges; residential treatment facilities; GPs and primary health care teams within the NHS; medical practitioners within the private sector; pharmacists; police, probation offers, prison staff, the Courts; national statistical offices; drug users; educationalists; health education; the media; research centres; those responsible for many different aspects of professional training; coroners; procurators fiscal; social services; mental health services; Drug Action Teams (DATs) and Drug and Alcohol Action Teams (DAATs).

A REPORT WITH VERY PRACTICAL INTENTIONS

1.17 Drug-related deaths pose for society a complex problem and one requiring careful analysis. We have therefore seen it as necessary in this report to give space to discussion of the nature of this problem and how best to measure its extent. Our aim is not, however, to conduct analysis for its own sake but to offer a report which is a strong catalyst for action, both in terms of reducing drug-related fatalities and improving the means for monitoring the scale of these deaths.

2 PATHOLOGY AND TOXICOLOGY OF IMMEDIATE DEATHS RELATED TO DRUG MISUSE

Characteristics of the drug, the route of use, and of the individual user help to explain why drugs used singly, in combination, or with alcohol, can act on many different body systems so as to cause death more or less immediately.

INTRODUCTION

IMMEDIATE DEATH FOLLOWING DRUG MISUSE

2.1   We use the term immediate death to describe those cases where death results directly from use of a drug, rather than from long term consequences of use. Many factors combine to lead to this outcome. This chapter will give an account of the mechanisms involved in the causation of immediate or near-immediate death from illicit drugs. It concentrates on the major causes and mechanisms of such deaths. Inevitably we are here going to use some technical terms but we will do our best to explain them as we go along.

THE SUBSTANCES WHICH WILL BE CONSIDERED

2.2   The following substances will be dealt with in turn: heroin, methadone, other opioids, cannabis, cocaine, Ecstasy, the benzodiazepines. Brief notes are given on amphetamine sulphate, LSD (lysergic acid diethlyamide) and volatile substances. Alcohol also receives attention. We discuss the highly important issue of drug interactions and multiple drug use as cause of death. We would, however, plead that sight not be lost of the fact that heroin misuse is today in this country the predominantly important cause of acute drug-related deaths.

THE NEED TO CONSIDER THE DIFFERENT POSSIBLE MECHANISMS OF DEATH

2.3   Among the many factors which determine whether an individual exposed to a particular substance will succumb to its toxicity, the pharmacological properties of the substance, together with the amount used, rank highly. In most cases they are the decisive factors responsible for death. Drugs can cause a critical interference with the function of vital organ systems which maintain life. As a basis for preventing drug-related deaths, it is essential to have an understanding of the precise mechanisms which may be implicated for each substance.

Table 2.1 Acute drug-related deaths: the drug, the route and the user.

FACTORS INVOLVED	COMMENT	CONTRIBUTION TO A FATAL OUTCOME
I The drug itself		
Nature of drug	The chemical structure is the main factor responsible for the toxicity of a drug.	+++
Dose of drug	Most toxic effects are dose-dependent, and a lethal outcome is most commonly attributable to the amount of drug taken.	+++
Purity of drug supply i) Inert contaminants (diluents)	Change in strength of supply may be responsible for some accidental deaths, but is not a major factor	+
ii) Toxic contaminants (intended as diluents)	Though highly publicised, toxicity due to contaminants is rare.	+/–
iii) Manufacturing error leading to a new toxic substance	This is a potential danger but most unusual in practice.	+/–
II The route of administration		
Intravenous	Potentially most toxic method due to rapid onset of peak levels of drug.	+++
Smoked / Inhaled	Gives a rapid effect. Heroin can be inhaled as vapour ("chasing the dragon"). Crack cocaine is inhaled as vapour.	+
Intranasal (snorting of powdered substance)	Gives a rapid effect, especially with cocaine.	+
Oral	Slower absorption and broken down by liver in many cases, therefore generally less toxic. Ingestion of a lethal dose is relatively easy (see 1).	++
III The individual		
Tolerance	Loss of tolerance plus use of previous customary dose appears to be an important factor in many opioid deaths.	+++
	Prescription or illicit sale of a "tolerant" dose of methadone to a naïve subject is an important and avoidable factor.	+++
Individual variation	Many drugs (e.g. methadone) have a large natural variation in their toxicity as between people.	++
Physical factors	Prolonged dancing without replacing fluid losses after taking ecstasy can cause hyperthermia. Water intoxication can occur in individuals who have taken ecstasy.	+
Illness	Physical illness may render drug use more hazardous.	+
Intention	The aim to obtain a greater "high" by using a larger dose involves a risk to life. Suicidal overdose is frequently successful, as the user knows the amount needed.	+

A FRAMEWORK

2.4   A useful framework within which to see much that we will discuss below on causes of immediate drug-related deaths involves the dimensions of drug, route of use, and characteristics of the user. That kind of perspective is represented in the mapping of the problem given in Table 2.1.

MAJOR TOXIC EFFECTS

LUNGS AND BREATHING

2.5   Direct depression of respiration, by a specific mechanism, such as depression by opioids of the centre in the brain which controls respiration, is the leading cause of immediate death. A generalised depression of the central nervous system can also have fatal consequences (as may occur with barbiturates, benzodiazepines or alcohol). If the victim is not breathing in enough oxygen, this can lead to a cardiac arrest and to low-oxygen brain damage.

2.6   Secondary effects may also occur when respiration is depressed. Blockage of the airways by saliva, mucus or vomit, can lead to a reduction in respiratory capacity below that required to maintain life. This usually only occurs when the level of consciousness and the cough reflex are depressed to a degree where the normal protective mechanisms do not operate. Secretions are permitted to accumulate, or vomit enters the airways. Acute respiratory distress due to conditions such as "crack lung" or opiate-induced asthma, can also be fatal.[1]

HEART

2.7   A reduction in the heart's output below that required to maintain life, apart from being a terminal event in many forms of illness and toxicity, is a cause of death in many forms of drug abuse. The reduction of cardiac output can be associated with direct or primary drug effects:

- cardiac depression (reduced contracting power of the heart leading to a fall in blood pressure and ultimately to collapse of the blood circulation system).

- cardiac arrhythmias (heart rhythm disturbances leading to a major fall or complete cessation of cardiac output).

- myocardial infarction (heart attacks may very rarely occur from acute spasm of the coronary arteries; but more commonly they result from accelerated coronary atheroma due to long-term use of stimulants, notably cocaine).

2.8   Reduction in cardiac output may also occur due to aspects of drug toxicity as a secondary effect:

- respiratory depression (which deprives the heart of oxygen, causing secondary cardiac depression, most typically with opioids).

- fluid volume depletion (due to extreme vasodilatation or sweating, most commonly in association with extreme rise in body temperature as typically may occur with stimulants)

- hyperthermia – (raised body temperature secondary to effects on heat production or to heat generation due to excessive muscular activity)

- hypothermia – (fall in body temperature usually in association with exposure to cold for a period of time – as may occur when a drug user is left collapsed and unconscious in a cold room or outdoors).

STROKES

2.9   The stimulant group of drugs (amphetamine, cocaine, Ecstasy) when taken in "recreational" doses tend to result in an acute rise in blood pressure which can be sufficient to cause a cerebrovascular accident (a term used to describe any kind of occurrence in which something untoward happens to blood vessels in the brain). This may be from an acute bleed (intracerebral haemorrhage or subarachnoid haemorrhage), or sometimes from thrombosis of cerebral arteries. More rarely, the same group of drugs can be associated with cerebral vasculitis (inflammation around blood vessels in the brain), which can reduce the flow of oxygenated blood and cause brain damage. Bleeding within the brain in particular can result in a fatal outcome.[2] The risk of such bleeds is much greater in people who have as congenital malformations small symptomless aneurysms ("berry" aneurysms), where the cerebral vessels branch.

2.10   Cerebrovascular accidents are likely to lead to a deficit in brain function which may be permanent (a "stroke"). Unless a good medical history is obtained and a history of drug misuse sought, the cause may not be recognised. The link between cerebrovascular accidents and cocaine is well described[3], while that with amphetamine and ecstasy is less widely known

LIVER

2.11   Cocaine and MDMA use may occasionally lead to liver failure, which can be fatal[4].

KIDNEY

2.12   Kidney failure can follow drug use, through a variety of mechanisms, which include an immunological reaction or a blood vessel illness. Kidney failure may also be due to rhabdomyolysis (damage to muscle tissue with release of breakdown products into the bloodstream) associated with raised body temperature (cocaine, MDMA), and it may occasionally occur with heroin.

INFECTIVE COMPLICATIONS

2.13   Intravenous drug use may result in virus infections which can be delayed in their consequences for many years, and those kinds of risk are dealt with in Chapter 9. But there are in addition a number of less common types of potentially fatal infective complications of drug misuse. These include septicaemia and infections which damage the valves of the heart (infective endocarditis). One study showed that intravenous drug users were 300 times more likely to die from infective endocarditis than non-intravenous users[5].

FATALITIES DUE TO ACCIDENTS OR VIOLENCE

2.14   All the drugs with which we are dealing in this chapter can in one way or another immediately impair mental functioning. They will therefore put the users (or other people) at risk of potentially fatal accidents. The most common dangers relate to driving and road traffic accidents. Many drugs, alone or in combination, can affect reaction time and co-ordination. There is also the danger of drug-induced impairment in judgement and a blurred sense of reality resulting in risky behaviour. How different drugs will in different circumstances affect different individuals will always be difficult to predict, and there is still much about the nature and extent of the fatal drug-accidents connection which is unknown.

2.15   As psychological depression is a common consequence of taking drugs, or of the drug taker's lifestyle, suicide often occurs in addicts. One study estimated that 8–17% of fatalities in heroin addicts were due to suicide.[6] Another aspect of drug taking is impaired judgement and sudden mood changes which can sometimes lead to aggression and violence. Coupled with the need to obtain money for addictive substances, violent crime (including domestic violence) and homicide can also be associated with drug taking but we would warn against exaggeration of this connection. Violent deaths may also occur as a result of drug dealing.

FACTORS WHICH INFLUENCE THE RISK ASSOCIATED WITH DRUG USE

MODE OF USE

2.16   Toxicity may be modified by the mode of use of a drug. When a drug is taken orally, the onset of effect tends to be gradual. When a drug is taken by injection, the blood levels peak rapidly and unconsciousness may occur more or less on the instant. The peak may exceed a potentially fatal level or trigger toxic mechanisms.

Inhalation of a drug, a relatively common method of use, whether by smoking so that the substance passes through the alveolar (lung) membrane, or by "snorting" so that the substance is absorbed through the lining of the nose, provides a rapid peak of drug levels. Smoked substances reach the brain quickly. With smoking there is also the potential problem of toxicity of products produced during combustion of the drug. This may be due to the substance itself or a contaminant. Fatal toxicity can occur with much lower doses after injection, smoking and inhalation than after oral consumption, and these routes are therefore more hazardous than when drugs are taken by mouth. Furthermore, damage to veins and arteries caused by injecting drugs can give rise to thrombosis which threatens life and causes death. Death may result from pulmonary embolus (clots moving to obstruct lung blood flow). In the case of injecting into an artery, damage to an arm, or more usually a leg, can if not treated surgically treated lead to infection and gangrene.

2.17   Both UK and international studies report that compared to the general population, injecting drug users are at increased risk of death from overdose; alcoholism; trauma; AIDS; infectious, circulatory, respiratory, and digestive diseases; violence; and unknown or ill-defined causes.

DRUG PURITY

2.18   Hammersley[7] concluded that an influx of exceptionally pure heroin alone could not explain an increase in drug deaths in Glasgow, although pure heroin mixed with other drugs might be implicated. Hall[8] has similarly argued that fatal heroin overdoses are probably only rarely a consequence of unexpectedly high purity, and that whilst variations in purity can cause overdoses, they appear to be a minor factor in causing fatal overdoses.

THE ROLE OF CONTAMINANTS

2.19   Street drugs tend to be diluted (cut) with inert substances intended as diluents or "fillers", or by other substances intended to modify the taste, appearance or effect of the drug. Death can ensue from the inclusion of a toxic substance by accident, or from an error in manufacture. Such fatalities are not however common, and the role of contaminants in drug-related deaths has sometimes been exaggerated. Much more usually it is the drug itself which kills.

THE SIGNIFICANCE OF DEPENDENCE AND TOLERANCE

2.20   Dependence to substances occurs when the brain adapts to repeated drug exposure and brain cells only fire in the presence of the drug. This is the basis for the withdrawal syndrome; a physiological reaction to drug withdrawal that can range from mild to life-threatening with different drugs (barbiturates and alcohol can give rise to particularly dangerous withdrawal states). In many drugs of misuse the dopamine system (dopamine is one of the body's naturally occurring chemical messengers) is involved in both dependence and withdrawal. This is, for instance, seen in the actions of cocaine on the nucleus accumbens, a small area of the brain which activates the dopamine reward system.

2.21   Heroin withdrawal produces a severe flu-like illness lasting up to 10 days. It is not fatal. Other opiates produce similar withdrawal states but of varying durations and intensities, but again they are not fatal. Withdrawal symptoms after benzodiazepine dependence are generally mild, but can be unpleasant and of long duration: if withdrawal from a benzodiazepine is abrupt after high doses have been used for a prolonged time, more severe symptoms, including convulsions and a delirium tremens like state may occur. Death is very unlikely on benzodiazepine withdrawal. Withdrawal from stimulant drugs such as cocaine and amphetamines can cause sleepiness, lack of energy and depression, but there are no marked physiological disturbances.

2.22   Repeated exposure to morphine results in less potent effect, that is, tolerance develops. For example, the initial dose of 10 mg of heroin escalates rapidly with regular use over as little as two weeks. The drug user who comes to an agency may be taking around 750 mg of street heroin daily. Tolerance begins to be lost immediately after cessation of use, and will be completely lost within two weeks of stopping the drug, so that a single dose of the amount previously taken has now become a potentially fatal overdose. Fatalities can occur among opioid users as a result of loss of drug tolerance, after a period of abstinence due to any cause.[9]

2.23   As for research on this topic, Shewan[10] investigated the likelihood of drug-related death amongst a sample of female drug users soon after release from prison. He concluded that the high proportion of fatal overdose deaths was likely to be related to the large number of drug users being held and then released. Consequently, the data did not seem to support the simple explanation that after release, individuals typically soon relapse to heroin use, and then overdose due to reduced tolerance. Contrary to this, Seaman[11] found that for injecting drug users infected with HIV, the risk of death from overdose during the 2 weeks after release from prison was 34 times higher than during other time spent outside prison. Findings from this study are more consistent with international research which suggests that overdose deaths are common among individuals who have lost tolerance.[12–13] Although much of the focus on loss of tolerance has concentrated upon release from prison as a possible risk factor, research in Italy provides a reminder that residential treatment of drug dependence may also be a situation where loss of tolerance can lead to increased risk of overdose[14].

SUBSTANCES

HEROIN (DIAMORPHINE)

2.24   Deaths from acute causes are common. Although respiratory depression is the commonest cause of death, there have been no reliable studies of the relative frequencies of different modes of death due to heroin, and one would expect these to vary over time. When Roberts and his colleagues[15] examined trends in death rates from accidental poisoning in teenagers aged 15–19 years from 1985–1995, they found that the largest single category of death from poisoning was accidental poisoning by opioids, which accounted for 21% (90/436) of the deaths recorded in the relevant ICD codes (this excludes deaths from VSA). A British study by Oppenheimer[16] which involved follow-up of 100 known users over a twenty year period, found them to have a mortality rate 14 times that of age-matched controls. Eskild followed up 200 injectors in Oslo and over a 36 month period found a 32 fold excess mortality[17]. In a study of non-fatal heroin overdose amongst heroin users recruited in non-clinical settings in London, Gossop[18] found that 9% of the 438 heroin users in their study reported at least one non-fatal overdose in the previous twelve months. A similar study by Taylor[19] of 1018 drug injectors recruited from Glasgow found that 27% reported at least one non-fatal overdose over a twelve month period. A study of 155 heroin users attending the Maudsley Hospital, London which was conducted on our behalf by Professor John Strang and Dr David Best is geographically limited but usefully topical. These investigations found that in the previous 12 months 43% had witnessed an average of 1.7 overdoses. Over their drug using careers (mean age now 36.1) 82.6% had witnessed an average of 5.6 overdoses of which 16.9% had resulted in death.

2.25   Mechanisms for heroin-related deaths include:

- Respiratory depression. This is the probable mode of death when a user is found dead with evidence of recent injection (a syringe still in the arm for instance, or other obvious signs of recent injection). However, death may not be instantaneous but a matter perhaps of the individual sliding into a deepening coma over some hours.

- Aspiration of vomit. This is sometimes found at post mortem, and is due to a combination of the emetic (vomiting) effect of heroin, combined with depression of the cough reflex.

- Pulmonary oedema (waterlogging of the lungs) due to injection of heroin, is a possible but uncommon cause of acute heroin-related fatality. The lungs are flooded by an outpouring of fluid and the person in effect drowns.

- Some of the fatalities that have resulted from heroin misuse may be due to an anaphylactoid reaction, that is to say an acute allergic response to the drug or its contaminants.[20]

- Heroin leucoencephalopathy (damage to the white matter of the brain) can occur after inhalation of vaporised heroin, but not after inhalation of powder or after injection of the drug. This complication, marked by progressive signs of brain impairment occurring over some time, was the cause of progressive neurological deterioration with 11 fatalities out of 47 cases reported from the Netherlands in 1981.[21] This neurotoxic effect is possibly due to a pyrolysis (thermal degradation) product of heroin or a contaminant. Sporadic cases have been reported elsewhere.

METHADONE

2.26 Methadone causes death in a similar manner to heroin (diamorphine). This topic is not dealt with further here, as it is the subject of Chapter 7.

OTHER OPIOIDS

2.27 There are number of pharmaceutical preparations containing opioids which may be obtained illegally and used by drug misusers. The principal drugs in this group are Diconal (dipipanone with cyclizine), Palfium (dextromoramide), DF118 (dihydrocodeine) and Temgesic (buprenorphine). Their pharmacological action is similar to heroin, and the side effects and mode of toxicity the same. In addition as they are marketed in tablet form, tablets are often ground up and injected. Diconal in particular causes a severe local inflammation, and blockage of the blood vessels into which it is injected. This may have serious consequences particularly if the drug is injected into a vein in the groin.

CANNABIS

2.28 There are no literature reports of acute death directly due to toxicity from cannabis. However, several reports have pointed to a statistical association between cannabis use and risk of road traffic accidents. In a study in the United States of 182 fatal truck accidents, 12.8% of drivers had used marijuana.[22] Williams *et al* reported a 36.8% incidence of cannabis use in fatally injured drivers in California.[23] A correlation has also been made between increased cannabis consumption and increased suicide rates.[24] Both in relation to road traffic accidents and suicides, we would however caution that neither presence nor correlation is the same as cause. In our view the causal significance of cannabis in relation to these kinds of deaths is still an open question. Cannabis may be found in blood or urine up to 28 days after last use or even longer, so positive laboratory findings at the time of an accident are only an uncertain indicator that the drug has been used at or near to the time of the accident (see paragraphs 4.41–42).

COCAINE

2.29   Cocaine is well known to have the potential for causing death, usually in relatively high recreational doses or in accidental overdose. The incidence of death in association with cocaine is currently in the UK much lower than that occurring in association with opioid misuse, but it is increasing and deserves attention. Heart and blood vessel deaths from cocaine use escalated in the United States during the 1980s as cocaine became purer, cheaper and easier to obtain.[25] The lethal effect is most commonly cardiac depression[26,27], which may be aggravated by exertion or arousal, or may occur in association with violent struggling which involves both of these. Severe toxicity is frequently accompanied by convulsions which may also aggravate the potential for heart toxicity by inducing hypoxia (depletion of oxygen in the body). Disturbance of the heart's rhythms and damage to the heart muscle have also been reported in some patients.[28,29,30] There is now ample evidence that cocaine use is associated with an increase in deaths from myocardial infarction. This is due to a combination of acute and chronic effects. Cocaine causes accelerated coronary atheroma, most probably due to repeated stresses on the cardiovascular system from the acute hypertensive effects of cocaine, and acute coronary spasm which is more likely to cause myocardial infarction when the vessels are damaged. Sudden cardiac death can also occur without evidence of myocardial changes or ischaemia, or with only minimal pathological changes in the heart.[30]

2.30   Chronic cocaine use appears to predispose patients with incidental or genetically determined abnormalities (aneurysms) in the blood vessels of the brain, to present with problems at an earlier point in their natural history than similar non-cocaine users.[31] Cocaine users can have significant atherosclerosis in their cerebral arteries.[32] Several studies, using PET scans and SPECT scans (brain imaging), have suggested that cocaine results in blood flow deficits in the brain which would be likely to cause local ischaemia (shortage of blood) and possibly local brain damage[33].

2.31   Cocaine can cause hypertension, rapid pulse rate and increased body temperature. High ambient temperature is associated with a significant increase in mortality from cocaine overdose.[34] Fatal overdoses have occurred in smugglers who have sought to secrete the drug by packing it in condoms, and then either swallowing it or packing it into the rectum. If a condom bursts, a fatal drug level will easily be achieved. One major complication of regular cocaine use is agitated delirium, in which over a short space of time the body overheats, the individual becomes agitated and paranoid, tears off their clothes and becomes violent and uncontrollable. Death frequently ensues, often while the sufferer is being restrained for their own and the public's safety.

2.32 To date there has been no UK research focusing specifically on cocaine overdoses. This probably reflects the fact that historically cocaine has not been central to the British illegal drug markets. In the US, however, where the misuse of cocaine-mainly in the form of cheap and highly addictive crack is considerably more widespread, research has tended to examine the role of cocaine more closely. For example, a 1988–1990 study of 699 crack and other cocaine users in Miami by Pottieger (1992)[35] found that a history of cocaine overdose was extremely common and that intravenous use was especially likely to result in overdose. Tardiff (1996)[36] found that of all accidental fatal overdoses (total 1,986) in New York City from 1990 to 1992, cocaine, often with opioids and ethanol, caused almost three-fourths of deaths, while opiates without cocaine caused roughly one-fourth of fatal overdoses. That cocaine is dangerous cannot be doubted.

ECSTASY

2.33 The use of "dance drugs" although relatively new in the UK, is now a cultural phenomenon. This is due to the introduction of the "Ecstasy" drugs, principally 3,4-methylenedioxymethamphetamine (MDMA) and related drugs, particularly 3,4-methylenedioxyethamphetamine (MDEA) and 3,4-methylenedioxyamphetamine (MDA). These drugs give rise to a small number of deaths in Britain each year. Deaths which occur soon after ingestion are usually due to cardiac arrhythmias, caused by the adrenaline-like properties of the drug. Hyperthermic collapse (overheating) is the commonest acute complication, due to dancing for long periods in a hot environment without adequate fluid replacement. This is largely due to the effect of the drug which enables the user to dance continuously without any feeling of tiredness or exhaustion, while at the same time suppressing the sensation of thirst. The result may be that the user becomes dehydrated, and loses the ability to lose heat by sweating and vasodilatation. The clinical pattern of toxicity in these cases includes potentially fatal hyperthermia (with body temperatures often in the region of 40–43°C), muscle tissue breakdown (sometimes leading to acute renal failure), and a condition known as disseminated intravascular coagulation in which there is widespread bleeding from the blood vessels. This drug is also capable of causing deaths from liver damage and from cerebrovascular accidents. Post mortem examination in MDMA-related fatalities may reveal widespread organ damage[37]. A few reports have linked MDMA (Ecstasy) use with non-fatal cerebrovascular accidents.[38]

2.34 So-called hyponatraemic collapse (hyponatraemia implies dilution of the blood), is an uncommon complication of MDMA which began to be reported from 1993 onwards. It appears to be partly due to a mistaken interpretation of harm limitation messages urging Ecstasy users to drink fluids. In these cases, the clinical pattern tends to be remarkably uniform, with initial vomiting and disturbed behaviour, followed by drowsiness, agitation and convulsions. Drowsiness, a mute state and disorientation, may persist for up to 3 days. In these cases, excess fluid ingestion is compounded by inappropriate secretion of antidiuretic hormone which is due to a pharmacological effect of the drug. The overall consequence is death by water intoxication.

BENZODIAZEPINES

2.35   Used properly within medical practice, the benzodiazepine class of drugs rightly enjoys the reputation of carrying a very low risk of death by accidental or intentional overdose. These drugs are in this regard much safer than the barbiturates which they have come almost entirely to replace as sedatives and sleeping tablets. The dependence potential of benzodiazepines means, however, that they should be used cautiously and in the short term only.

2.36   Besides their legitimate use in clinical practice, benzodiazepines have today become in Britain widespread drugs of misuse. Different benzodiazepines carry different levels of danger but all can cause fatal respiratory depression, particularly so if tablets are ground up and injected or when benzodiazepines are taken in conjunction with opioids and alcohol. Temazepam has been widely misused, but more recently in some parts of the country diazepam (Valium), is causing major problems. We feel that the risk of death resulting from misuse of these drugs, and their potential for adverse or even fatal interactions, has somewhat slipped from awareness. This has resulted in the too great willingness of doctors to prescribe benzodiazepines to their drug misusing patients on a continuous basis, with consequent risks of diversion (see Chapter 8). Benzodiazepines can, when taken with alcohol or opioids, all too easily give rise to fatal overdose.

ALCOHOL AS CAUSE OF DEATH

2.37   We have in a previous ACMD report (Drug Misuse and the Environment) emphasised our belief that in broad terms prevention of alcohol-related problems and of problems relating to illicit drugs, cannot always be separated at the practical level. Problems of use overlap, and fatal mechanisms can also interact.

2.38   The popular view of alcohol-related deaths probably still centres on chronic physical diseases such as cirrhosis of the liver, and mortality among the middle-aged or elderly sectors of the population. In fact, alcohol is also a significant cause of death among young people. The mechanisms include poisoning by alcohol overdose, inhalation of vomit, alcohol-induced lowering of blood sugar, and deaths by road traffic accident, and other types of accident and violence. Among the older population those same causes contribute to acute alcohol-related mortality, but acute deaths due to cardiac arrhythmia, stroke, acute pancreatitis and gastro-intestinal bleeding, also need to be taken into the reckoning.

OTHER DRUGS

AMPHETAMINE SULPHATE

2.39   Amphetamine use leads to an increase in heart rate and blood pressure, and can cause strokes. It can also result in cardiac arrhythmias, cardiovascular collapse and death. Hyperthermia and convulsions can rarely also be fatal. Thus its toxic effects are in many ways similar to those of cocaine. However, despite relatively widespread use, deaths are rare but appear to be increasing. A few reports in the international literature highlight the role of accidents, particularly traffic accidents, and suicides in the deaths of amphetamine users. This, commentators suggest, results from the bizarre and reckless behaviour that may result from the drug-induced "high", and from the circumstances in which it is commonly used.[39-40]

LYSERGIC ACID DIETHYLAMIDE (LSD)

2.40   Deaths due to a direct toxic effect of LSD are virtually unknown, but there are anecdotal cases of fatal road traffic accidents, and of falling to death from high places. LSD may also be associated with unpredictable and sometimes violent behaviour towards self and others.

VOLATILE SUBSTANCES

2.41   We dealt with causes of deaths related to volatile substance abuse in a previous ACMD report[41] and will not repeat those details here. We must however note that VSA continues to be a significant cause of acute deaths among young people, and we will return to issues of prevention in a later chapter. From 1970 to 1990 the number of deaths occurring each year in the UK from VSA rose steadily, peaking at 152 in 1990. Annual totals decreased over the subsequent four years to 65 deaths in 1994, probably at least in part because of a Department of Health publicity campaign initiative. They then rose again in 1995 (73 deaths) and 1996 (79 deaths), although falling back slightly in 1997 to 73 deaths.[42] This recent upward trend, although not statistically significant, is worrying. One would rather have seen a further fall.

MULTIPLE SUBSTANCES

2.42   Drug misuse is rarely confined to a single substance. When an individual takes two substances in sub-lethal amounts, the combination may be capable of causing death if they affect similar body functions. Even if, for example, opioids and benzodiazepines depress respiration by different methods, this effect can combine to convert an otherwise sub-lethal amount of each drug into a fatal combination (see 2.30). Studies have shown the simultaneous consumption of heroin and benzodiazepines places individuals at a particularly high risk of overdose. Hammersley[7] reported that heroin, often mixed with other drugs which most often included temazepam, diazepam and alcohol, was implicated in the increase in drug-related deaths in Glasgow between 1990 and 1992. Furthermore, buprenorphine-benzodiazepine mixtures seemed much less likely to lead to fatal overdose than heroin-benzodiazepine mixtures, or heroin alone[43]. Even small amounts of alcohol will increase the risk with heroin.[44]

2.43   Drugs of misuse are, as mentioned above, often taken at the same time as alcohol. In the human liver, cocaine and alcohol are combined to form cocaethylene, which intensifies the euphoric effects of cocaine but which may also increase the risk of sudden death. This substance has been found in post mortem blood, liver and nervous system tissue in amounts which may exceed those of cocaine.[45] But the types of interaction between alcohol and other drugs which may be involved in acute drug-related deaths are various.

2.44   In summary, every drug combination that occurs in the course of drug misuse adds to the dangers, is unpredictable in its consequences, and may all too easily lead to tragedy. Users are repeatedly inflicting on themselves types of pharmacological experiment which no doctor would dare carry out.

2.45   Clinicians should be aware of the many types of interactions which can occur between prescribed and illicit drugs. Useful guidance is given in the British National Formulary.

CONCLUSIONS

2.46   This chapter has sought to provide a scientific basis for understanding why and how drugs can acutely kill their users. As stated in the opening paragraph, we believe these kinds of insight can inform the needed prevention policies. Beyond the directly instrumental implications of this science for prevention, we would however also suggest that a reading end-to-end of the facts laid out here may serve as a corrective to any view of drugs as no more than symbols, fun, or recreational substances. Drugs can kill, suddenly and often unexpectedly. They can do so in many different and interacting ways which can overwhelm many different body systems and leave people dead.

3 SOCIAL, SITUATIONAL, AND PERSONAL FACTORS WHICH MAY CONTRIBUTE TO RISK OF DEATH ASSOCIATED WITH DRUG MISUSE

This chapter seeks to identify the characteristics of people most at risk of death from drug misuse. That kind of information will help target preventive action.

INTRODUCTION

3.1   The previous chapter dealt with the dangers to the individual of drugs as drugs, within the toxicological perspective. Building on that discussion, we now proceed to an analysis which acknowledges that drug misuse is an individual behaviour which occurs within a social context. An understanding of personal and social factors that bear on the risk of a fatal toxicological outcome or virus transmission, will contribute further and usefully to the broad understandings needed to strengthen prevention.

3.2   Perhaps the first point to note here is that there have been relatively few distinctly sociological studies on the topic of drug-related death. In the nineteen sixties and seventies social scientists were interested in the processes underlying the labelling of certain deaths as "suicide". More recently attention has focussed upon the social processes of death certification[1]. Throughout most of the nineteen eighties and early nineteen nineties, much of the attention of social scientists working in the addictions field was directed at HIV infection. Early research of this trend focussed upon such topics as establishing the prevalence of injecting drug use, identifying the frequency with which injecting drug users shared injecting equipment, and identifying the frequency with which injecting drug users had unprotected sexual contact. It was only in the latter stages of this research that sociological work was undertaken into such topics as, for example, the determinants of drug injectors' risk behaviour, the social meaning of needle and syringe sharing, and the place of risk-taking more generally within the everyday world of injecting drug users.

3.3   Alongside a reduction in behavioural research on HIV, there has recently been a marked increase in research on drug-related deaths. In a similar way to the behavioural research on HIV, much of the initial research on this topic has had a clear medical focus. It has, for example, sought to identify the extent of drug-related deaths, the role of different drugs in such deaths, the impact of loss of tolerance, and the effects of drug combinations.

3.4   By and large we are not yet at the stage where sociological research has been undertaken on such topics as, for instance, drug injectors' attitudes towards overdose and drug-related deaths, individual strategies for reducing the risk of death and drug overdose, and drug users' reactions to overdose. Nor do we fully understand the way in which factors such as gender, age, and social class may impinge upon injectors' behaviour so as to increase the risk of death. Research in these areas is however now beginning to take place.

3.5   As a result of the current state of research there is therefore rather less in this review chapter of a social science kind than one might have expected. Nonetheless, there is some very interesting and policy relevant research which can be identified and it is on this which we will now report.

USER CHARACTERISTICS

GENDER

3.6   Most UK and international studies report higher drug-related mortality rates for men than for women. The review of drug-related deaths reported by coroners in England and Wales, reported a male:female ratio of 3.8:1[2]. In a survey of deaths of chronic drug abusers who came to medico-legal autopsy in the South-east of Scotland, the ratio was 6.1:1. VSA deaths are also more common among males than females.[3] The 1997 ratio was 3.3:1, having been around 7.2:1 for the period 1971–1995.

3.7   Some qualifications regarding this gender difference are, however, required. Attention needs to be directed at the relative size of the using population (denominator) as well as the number of deaths (numerator). Thus, in their study of deaths among opioid dependent subjects in the Brighton Health District, O'Doherty and Farrington[4] noted that the finding of 47 male deaths versus 13 female deaths, obscured the actual doubled rate of death among female compared to male drug dependency unit attenders. Similarly, Frischer[5] found that whilst male injectors in Glasgow were 1.4 times more likely to die than their non-injecting counterparts, female injectors were over 4 times more likely to die. Oppenheimer and her colleagues[6] found no sex differences in mortality rates among the 43 people who died over a 22 year follow-up period of a cohort of 128 heroin addicts. However, it is important to recognise that the research in this area has been largely correlational in identifying a statistical relationship between the two variables of drug-related death, and gender. What such research has not been able to do is to identify those aspects of male and female gender, which might explain why drug-related deaths should generally appear to be a greater risk for males, compared to females.

AGE

3.8   Studies consistently report that the majority of deaths by volatile substance abuse are of young people in their mid to late teens[7]. The pattern of death by age for other drugs is not quite so consistent, but on the whole research tends to show that deaths are more likely to occur amongst individuals in their twenties (see 6.4). In the study by Ghodse[8], the median age at death was 33 years. The Oppenheimer study[6] reported that among heroin addicts the observed mortality rates increased with age, although the excess mortality was concentrated at the younger ages. According to Bentley and Busuttil[9], the peak age at death of chronic drug misusers was in the third decade of life.

3.9   The association between age and risk of drug-related death is likely to be in part a function of the length of time the individual has been using drugs. However, it is also likely to be the case that amongst neophyte users who have little knowledge of drug concentrations, there may be an increased risk of overdose. Equally there may be an association between the length an individual has been using illegal drugs, the development of a pattern of dependent drug use and an increasing sense of despair at the individual's circumstances, which may increase the risk of suicidal thoughts. Thus these linked factors of age and length of time using illegal drugs may exert an influence in their own right, but they also provide an increasing opportunity for all sorts of other factors to intervene that may have an impact on an individual's risk of drug-related death. The relationship between age and drug-related death is likely to be a good deal more complicated than might appear at first, and it would be wrong to assume that it is only or specially the novice user who is at risk.

EMPLOYMENT, INCOME AND SOCIAL CLASS

3.10   Drug deaths tend to be more common amongst unemployed and unskilled workers. In the study by Ghodse[8], 49% of individuals who died were unemployed, whilst the survey of 62 drug deaths in Glasgow identified an even higher degree of unemployment (91%)[10]. The data we give in Chapter 6 (paragraph 6.7) which show the relationship in England and Wales between social deprivation and drug-related deaths should also be noted. Data from Scotland show a remarkable correlation between non-psychiatric hospital admissions related to drug misuse and levels of socio-economic deprivation as measured by the Carstairs deprivation score (Figure 3.1) (Reference: The Scottish Office: Tackling Drugs in Scotland : Action in Partnership, Edinburgh 1999). There are nearly four times as many deaths from VSA in social class V compared with other social classes, and areas with high VSA death rates have high levels of deprivation.[11] Although the UK literature discussing drug deaths, employment, income and social class is limited, it is consistent with international findings.[12–14]

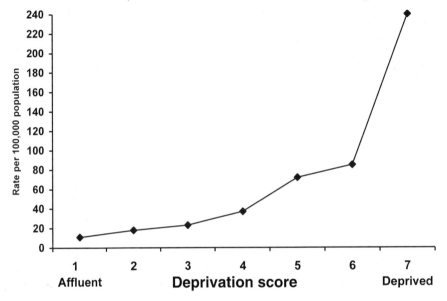

Figure 3.1 Non-psychiatric hospital admissions related to drug misuse in Scotland 1996-98 by deprivation score of patients' place of residence

3.11   The relationship between these environmental variables and drug-related deaths is likely to be far from straightforward. Problematic drug misuse, including drug injecting, is itself highly influenced by these factors. Moreover the relationship between such factors as income, social class, and problematic drug misuse is not one way; developing a pattern of dependent drug use or drug injecting is itself likely to exert an influence upon the level of an individual's income and their capacity to remain in employment. But a reasonable conclusion might be that drug-related deaths are often causally embedded in a complicated and as yet not fully understood nexus of adverse social context.

MENTAL HEALTH STATUS, DEPRESSION AND SUICIDE

3.12   Poor mental health, particularly depression, is a key factor predisposing individuals to suicide. Physical illness, poor family relationships, social isolation, and stressful life events, also increase the likelihood of suicide. Since all of these are associated with drug misuse, it is unsurprising that individuals with a history of drug problems often take their own lives. Bentley and Busuttil[9] reported that 16 (9%) of drug-related deaths in their study were the result of suicide. Crighton and Towl[15], provided a detailed analysis of self inflicted deaths in prison custody and found that drug users were over-represented, with 29% of those who killed themselves having had a history of drug misuse. This compared with estimated rates of drug use for the prison population of around 11.5%.

3.13 There is also some evidence to suggest that HIV infection and AIDS add to suicidal risk.[16–18] The incidence of psychiatric co-morbidity and suicidality among drug users, including methadone maintained clients, has not been well researched in the UK, but has been highlighted in the international literature, particularly in the USA.[19–20]

LOCATION

3.14 According to Ghodse and his team[2], the highest drug-related death rates per 100,000 population were reported by 8 of the 96 coroners' jurisdictions which they studied. These were: Blackpool and Fylde, Brighton & Hove, Inner London (North), Lincoln, Norwich, Peterborough, Pembrokeshire and Reading. The extent to which this reflects reporting habits as opposed to actual incidence is uncertain. Where place of death was reported, 68% of individuals died in a residence, 25.9% died in hospital, and 6% died in other locations, for instance public toilets. In Glasgow, Cassidy[10] noted that the majority of deaths occurred near centres of known supply. Furthermore, although a number occurred in the family home, a large proportion were not at the place of residence. In respect of VSA, the place where the substance was abused prior to death has been fairly evenly divided between indoors, and public places such as parks and shopping centres.[3,21] Although VSA is a national problem, it has an uneven geographical distribution, with death rates highest in the northern areas of the United Kingdom.[3]

HOMELESSNESS

3.15 Although Ghodse[8] reported that only 4.6% of his sample were without fixed abode, British research has not to-date focused on any additional risk of mortality amongst homeless drug users. Data from Hamburg[22], however, showed that approximately one-third of all drug-related deaths in 1991 occurred in users who were without housing. The injection of drugs in public places was identified as a risk factor in causing overdose in Paris.[23] This was because the drug would have to be injected quickly and without caution, and this would increase the risk of toxic accidents. Consistent with this argument, Gutierrez-Cebollada[24] found that the self-injection of heroin in an unusual place, was a risk factor for heroin overdose in Barcelona. We think that this non-UK literature probably carries relevance for this country, and here too homelessness and injecting outdoors are likely to be risk factors.

DRUG AVAILABILITY

3.16   Although there is no UK literature specifically considering the impact of drug availability on the incidence of drug-related deaths, international research suggests that the incidence of use or misuse of any substance largely reflects the availability of that substance. One aspect of availability is price. According to Hyatt and Rhodes[25], there was a significant negative relationship between the estimated street price of cocaine and the level of related medical emergencies and deaths due to misuse of this drug. As is true of the demand for other products, the demand for cocaine was, in other words, sensitive to its price. Consistent with the availability argument, Howard[26] found that deaths due to barbiturate poisoning in a metropolitan area in the USA, decreased with the decreased prescribing of those drugs, while benzodiazepine-related deaths increased with the increased availability of those substances. The curtailment of the heroin epidemic in that same area during the mid 1970s reflected drug misuse treatment and prevention programmes, and a concentrated effort by enforcement officials at restricting the flow and sale of heroin. We think that this international literature is, in broad terms, likely to bear on the problems in this country. If availability of drugs decreases, deaths due to the relevant drugs are likely to decrease. But at present one cannot go beyond an assertion of likelihood. Drug-related deaths could decrease even if there was an increase in the use of less harmful drugs, or an increase in the use of drugs in less harmful ways.

RISK PERCEPTION AND RISK RESPONSE AMONGST DRUG USERS

3.17   It is important to understand drug users' own assessments of their risk of overdose. Such assessments are likely to influence their reactions to overdose and the probability of their adopting strategies aimed at reducing that risk. However, this is not a topic that has been widely studied to date. Although useful information in this area is beginning to emerge, for the time being we again have to rely on overseas findings. For instance, in a recent Australian study, Darke and Ross[27] found that of 312 heroin users surveyed only 20% believed that they were likely to overdose in the future, 30% thought that this was unlikely and 50% thought it very unlikely. And 77% of drug users said that they rarely or never worried about overdose. This was despite the fact that these subjects estimated that 60% of heroin users would experience an overdose in their heroin-using career. Whilst it might have been thought that witnessing an overdose would exert a positive influence on drug users' assessments of risk, in fact the authors of this research found no such clear relationship.

3.18   Although from an outsider's perspective it might be assumed that drug users and in particular drug injectors, would inevitably be concerned with the risk of overdose, in fact this is not necessarily the case. Using interviews and focus groups with illicit drug users, Rhodes[28] concluded that everyday heroin use is permeated by risks. There are risks of dependence; overdose; HIV or hepatitis transmission; injecting damage; using bad heroin; risks related to buying and dealing and going to jail. Thus, for many drug users, the risk of overdose is likely to be a relatively small concern, part of the routine danger of using street heroin, and not an unusual occurrence.

3.19   Building on this theory, Rhodes[29] subsequently explored how risk behaviour is socially organised among drug users. He concluded that such behaviour is the outcome of a complex interplay between individual and social factors. Behaviours which are, for public health reasons, considered 'risky', may be viewed in different terms by drug users themselves. Without understanding how drug users perceive and behave in response to risk, it is not possible fully to appreciate why it is that they behave as they do, and why it is that they may continue to engage in behaviours they know to carry a risk.

3.20   The reactions of drug users to overdose is particularly important in view of the finding[30] that many drug deaths occur in the company of other drug users. Zador et al[31] reported that, in their study, 58% of overdose cases occurred while other people were present. In a study by Walsh[32] the figure was 79%. In the research reported by Manning[33] in 1983, more than half of the overdoses occurred with others present. In only 23% of the cases of overdose reported by Manning did the individual collapse immediately. In over half of the cases reported by Garriet and Sturner[34], an interval of more than 3 hours elapsed before medical assistance was sought. In the study by Nakamura[35] in 1978, 44% of cases had an interval greater than 2 hours before help was sought. Manning found that in 42% of cases help was acquired 3 hours after final injection and after other remedies, such as a cold shower, had been tried. On the basis of such findings one would have to conclude that there is considerable potential to intervene at an earlier point in drug-related emergencies than may generally be occurring at the moment, with a reduction in the likelihood of a fatal outcome on at least some occasions.

3.21   Researchers are also beginning to look at drug injectors' attempts at reducing their risk of overdose. Darke and Ross[36] found in Australia that 73% of injectors said that they did things to reduce their risks of overdose; 20% said that they rarely injected heroin after having used alcohol; 54% said that they never consumed alcohol in conjunction with heroin. However, 5% said that they always combined these drugs. Injecting on one's own is likely to carry a particularly high risk, because of the reduced likelihood of someone discovering the overdose and alerting medical services. But 52% of injectors in Darke and Ross's study reported having injected alone, and 10% said that they always injected alone.

CONCLUSIONS

3.22   In the opening paragraph to this chapter we suggested that drug use is behaviour which occurs within a social context. The complexities hidden in that word "context" have become apparent as this exposition has proceeded. For instance, some of the context is the individual's age and gender and length of drug use. Background factors such as employment, income, social class and social deprivation may be relevant. Virus status and mental health bear on individual vulnerability to suicide. There is the immediate physical and social context which will or will not offer support if overdose occurs: a cold room or a heated flat; a friend present or run away. And within this nexus there is the individual using a more or less dangerous drug by a route of use carrying lesser or greater risk, and with that individual making an accurate or blithely inaccurate personal appraisal of the riskiness of their drug-taking.

3.23   We believe that what we have summarised of this chapter in the paragraph above, amply supports the contention that although drugs are a prime cause of drug-related deaths, the totality of a complex personal and social context (the person within a contextual background and foreground), also has to be taken into the reckoning if we are to build intelligent prevention policies. Prevention of drug-related deaths must deal with drugs but be sensitive to the wider realities.

4 THE PRESENT SYSTEM FOR COLLECTING DATA ON DRUG DEATHS AND PROBLEMS WITHIN THEM

The availability of credible data on drug-related deaths is of great importance. Regrettably, the current system for generating these data is flawed. We describe that system and identify the multiple problems within it.

THE APPROACH WHICH WE TAKE

4.1 Chapters 4, 5 and 6 are closely linked and they all bear on the issue of data. Chapter 4 describes the relevant current data system in different countries within the UK, and identifies the problems. Chapter 5 makes suggestion for improvement, and Chapter 6 gives some key selected output available from present sources.

4.2 To have in place a system which can year-on-year generate trustworthy data on drug-related deaths is of fundamental importance to the national drugs strategy. Without such data the policy process will be in the dark as to how often what drugs are causing death to what people, and in what circumstances. There will be no confident ability to monitor trends over time, and no basis for assessing the efficiency of policies directed at reducing these deaths. Good data are here, and as ever, the foundation of good public health.

4.3 Such data are in this instance important because they enumerate these deaths, describe their correlation, and provide the basis for monitoring the efficiency of policies targeted at their prevention. We see this as their prime contribution, rather than their providing a reliable indirect indicator of the size of the overall drug problem. It is possible to envisage drug-related deaths going up while the national prevalence of drug misuse went down, and vice versa.

4.4 As an essential first step we have attempted to develop a detailed understanding of how the present system work. We admit that we have at times felt somewhat baffled by that question. It is not only a matter of understanding how the system operates in theory, but also of how a linked system of personal and professional interpretations of administrative rules and intentions works out in practice. This is a system which has grown incrementally, rather than having a strong coherence and with everyone serving one common intention. That may have been a satisfactory state of affairs when there were only a few drug-related deaths each year, but it is inadequate for the accurate monitoring of what has become a major public health problem.

4.5   The intention must be to capture all deaths where, on a reasonable balance of probabilities, one or more stated substance is in some degree implicated in the cause of the individual's death. We do not aim for certainty but only at reasonable probability.

4.6   The substances with which this report is most directly concerned are illicit drugs. Volatile solvent abuse deaths should also be captured within the system. Deaths related to over-the-counter medications are not our direct concern. The system must succeed in distinguishing between deaths due to those substances and due to illicit drugs, but we believe that their reporting can be contained as separate data within the same framework. Alcohol is not the primary concern of this report, but its interactions with illicit drugs are of such importance as to persuade us that there is a case for again trying to get it within the same general reporting frame as we will be proposing. The implications of these suggestions would however, require consideration by some group other than ourselves. We are well aware that alcohol-related deaths have their own recording complexities.

4.7   Within the perspectives of this report at least the following major underlying types of 'relatedness' then have to be considered as cutting across the different substance-related causes:

• Deaths due to acute poisoning whether accidental or self intended, or due to drug-related acute illness

• Deaths due to chronic illnesses

• Deaths due to road traffic accidents

• Deaths of victims due to an intentional poisoning by some other party

We see 4.5–4.7 as representing the core perspective expressed within the present system, and it should be preserved.

THE CURRENT SYSTEM AND ITS PROBLEMS: ENGLAND AND WALES

4.8   What we will do in this section is go through the present system step by step, and at each step seek to identify any implicit problems. In Table 4.1 a summary of those problems is given. In describing the current system we seek to describe their essentials rather than going into every administrative detail. Different parts of the United Kingdom have in this arena somewhat different administrative systems in place (that is part of the problem), and we start here with England and Wales. Figure 4.1 summarises the basic steps.

Table 4.1 Problems within the present data collection system on England and Wales collection system on deaths related to drug misuse. References to appropriate paragraphs are given in brackets

Deaths due to chronic virus diseases are not captured (4.9)

The coroner's fundamental responsibility is not that of collecting public health data (4.11)

A post mortem does not necessarily include a toxicological examination (4.12)

The choice of verdicts open to the coroner when recording a drug-related death are unsatisfactory and confusing (4.15).

The information which is gathered on the drugs involved in the death may be incomplete (4.18)

The coroner's certificate gives no indication as to whether a toxicological examination was carried out (4.18)

The certificate gives no indication as to whether injected drug misuse was involved (4.18)

The criteria which will lead a coroner to request a toxicological examination are unclear (4.18)

ONS appears to have no routine way of checking back with the coroner's office if information is incomplete (4.22)

The coding frame used by ONS which mirrors the coroner's approach is similarly unsatisfactory (4.23)

The current ONS approach to reporting drug-related deaths is unsatisfactory for our purposes in that it also will capture cases other than drug-misuse related deaths (4.27)

There are some unnecessary variations in the recording of drug-related deaths across the constituent parts of the UK (4.36)

The problem of how to get data on the involvement of drug misuse in road traffic accidents has not been resolved (4.41–4.43)

CDSC and SCIEM tracking of drug-related deaths is incomplete (4.46)

International comparisons on rates of drug-related deaths are at present likely to be unreliable (4.50)

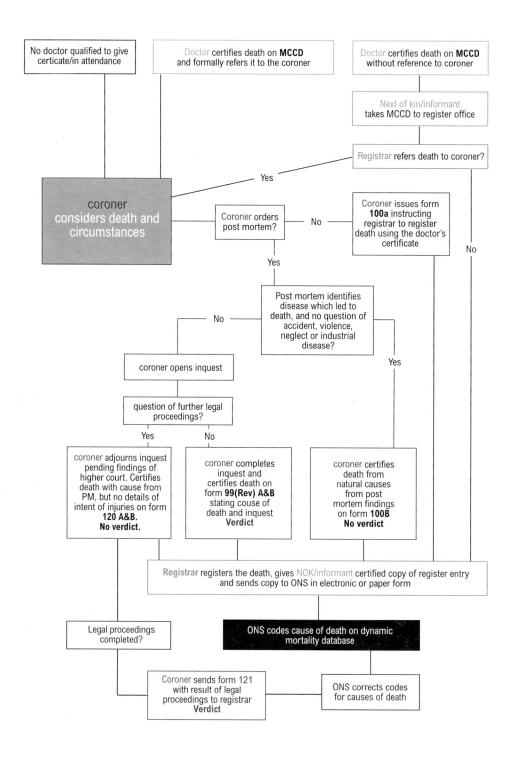

Figure 4.1 Process of collecting and coding cause of death data, England and Wales

DOCTORS NOTIFY THE CORONER

4.9   Doctors traditionally see it as their duty to refer deaths to coroners when appropriate although strictly speaking responsibility lies with the Registrars of Births Deaths and Marriages. The statutory requirement is that the Registrar will report deaths to the coroner if

- the deceased was not attended during his last illness by a medical practitioner;

- a duly completed certificate of cause of death cannot be obtained;

- the deceased was not seen after death, nor within 14 days before death, by the certifying medical practitioner;

- the cause of death appears unknown;

- the death appears to be unnatural, caused by violence or neglect, abortion, or attended by suspicious circumstances;

- the death appeared to have occurred during an operation or before recovery from the effects of an anaesthetic; or

- the death appears to have been due to industrial disease or poisoning.

In turn, coroners are required to hold an inquest if the death was due to violence, unnatural, or sudden and of unknown cause. (They must also hold inquests into deaths in prison.) The registrar is thus required to report a rather wider selection of cases than will necessarily result in an inquest in the interests of ensuring, as far as possible, that deaths which might need to be subject to an inquest can be considered by the coroner. However, as mentioned, in practice most doctors know what sort of deaths will be reportable to coroners and by-pass the registrar by contacting the coroner themselves, saving time in the interests of the deceased's relatives. They may not include deaths due to HIV or hepatitis where the deceased may be known to have contracted the disease through injecting drug use many years previously.

4.10   Doctors are trained from their earliest professional days to take the need to notify the coroner seriously and will probably err on the side of caution. Deliberate failures by a GP or hospital practitioner to notify acute drug-related deaths to the coroner are therefore likely to be rare, although a doctor might be unaware of the drug involvement in some instances of death.

THE CORONER

4.11   The coroner's primary function is to establish the circumstances and cause of death and to investigate the possibility of any criminal involvement. Compiling statistical data is a secondary concern, although some coroners are known to have a particular interest in drug-related deaths. There are 138 coroners in England

and Wales, of which about 25 are full time, including the seven coroners in London. Many of the rest are solicitors who act as coroners part-time. There is considerable variation between coroners in terms of facilities, resources and workloads. Coroners have to decide their verdicts in the light of the evidence presented at the inquest and in the exercise of their judicial discretion. They also have discretion in deciding what information they record on the coroner's certificate of cause of death. The result can be the immediate and evident problem that there are coroners working in areas of known high drug prevalence who never certify a death as related to drug misuse.

4.12   The coroner generally orders a post mortem to be carried out by a pathologist. The post mortem may, but does not necessarily, include a toxicological examination, and we return to this issue shortly (para 4.20).

4.13   The coroner or coroner's officer (often a retired police officer), then collects additional information on the deceased, from various sources such as the police, medical records, relatives, friends and any available witnesses. This may include information on the drug history of the deceased although this can be difficult to collect. For example, relatives are often unaware of, or are unwilling to give details on, the deceased's drug habits. Similarly, where witnesses are also drug users, they may be reluctant to supply information on the deceased's drug use for fear of being implicated in the death.

4.14   Following the post mortem, the coroner may hold an inquest, which will normally be held without a jury. The coroner takes into account the pathologist's report if there is one, together with the findings of their own investigations. He or she then decides the cause, or causes, of death and gives a verdict. In the case of drug-related deaths, the coroner has a choice of six alternative and mutually exclusive verdicts:

> Dependence on drugs
>
> Non-dependent abuse of drugs
>
> Accident/misadventure
>
> Suicide
>
> Lawful killing
>
> Unlawful killing
>
> Open (only to be used where there is insufficient evidence to record any other verdict)

4.15   We believe that the above framework is for several reasons inadequate for purposes of systematic data collection.

- It is unreasonable to expect a coroner to distinguish between "Dependence on drugs" and "Non-dependent abuse of drugs".

- The first two choices are not logically alternatives to any of the four which follow, but potentially complementary.

- This rubric gives potential for the drug-relatedness of a death to go unrecorded.

4.16   Having completed the inquest, the coroner certifies the death. Where both a post mortem and an inquest have been carried out, which is the case for virtually all deaths which are known to be drug-related including suicides and accidents (over 99 per cent between 1993 and 1996), the coroner certifies the death using Form 99 (Rev) (Appendix C). Alternative forms are used if there is no inquest or if the inquest is adjourned pending criminal proceedings (ONS Series DH4).

4.17   In addition to general details on the deceased such as name, age, sex, date of death, occupation, usual address, cause(s) of death and marital status, the coroner's certificate also contains information on whether a post mortem was held and the coroner's verdict. In the case of deaths by accident or misadventure, Part V of Form 99 (Rev) (Appendix 1) requires the coroner to supply details of where and how the "accident" happened. This section may also be completed for non-accidental deaths, but is not obligatory.

4.18   In the cause of death section of the certificate, the coroner may mention any drugs identified but this is not a requirement. Where more than one substance is recorded, there is usually no indication of the relative quantities, or which substance was likely to be responsible for the death. Often only a general description, such as 'drug overdose', is recorded; this is the case in around 10 per cent of deaths attributed to drugs. In some cases this may be because the coroner only received the pathologist's report just before the inquest. The coroner's certificate generally does not include any indication of whether a toxicological examination was carried out nor on the route(s) of drug administration.

4.19   We see it as unsatisfactory that the recording of important matters relating to the role of drugs in the cause of deaths should thus, in effect, be left to a voluntary and unstructured annotation on a report form.

POST MORTEM TOXICOLOGICAL EXAMINATIONS

4.20   As mentioned above (4.12), a coroner may or may not request a toxicological examination at the time when a post mortem is performed. We found no way of discovering the criteria which effect this choice, the consistency with which those criteria are applied nationally, or the range of tests likely to be requested. We suspect that in general post mortem testing for the presence of drugs is only performed at the coroner's specific request and in the following circumstances:–

- When there is strong presumptive evidence that a sudden death is drug-related, and confirmation is being sought as to the substances involved.

- Screening for drugs when the death is a suspected suicide.

- Somewhat uncertainly, screening for drugs where death is due to a road traffic accident. This is not routine.

- Screening where the cause of death is obscure.

THE REGISTRAR OF BIRTHS AND DEATHS

4.21   The coroner's certificate is sent to the registrar of births and deaths, who registers the death using the information on the certificate, together with details from an informant where no inquest has been carried out. The registrar does not receive the reports made by the pathologist or the police.

OFFICE FOR NATIONAL STATISTICS (ONS)

4.22   ONS receives only the information on the registration form, together with Part V of the coroner's certificate. Since 1993 the information on the death certificate has been stored electronically on the ONS mortality database (ONS 1996). So far as we can discover, ONS has no routine way of checking back with the coroner's office if information is incomplete. However, when ICD10 is introduced in 2001, medical enquiries may be undertaken once again.

4.23   From this information and working within set rules, the officer concerned will code up all causes of death mentioned on the death registration form, according to the Ninth Revision of the International Classification of Diseases (ICD9)[1]. There are five main groups of ICD9 codes which cover deaths directly due to drugs:

304	Drug dependence
305	Non-dependent abuse of drugs
E850–E858	Accidental poisoning by drugs, medicaments and biologicals
E950	Suicide and self-inflicted poisoning by solid or liquid substances
E980	Poisoning by solid or liquid substances, undetermined whether accidentally or purposely injected

In addition, a small number of deaths may be attributed to assault by poisoning (ICD9 E962), or to drug psychoses (ICD9 292). Deaths attributed to ICD9, 292, 304 and 305 may be processed by the automatic coding system. All other codes, including external cause, are allocated by members of ONS staff.

4.24   We see this approach as logically unsatisfactory for much the same reasons as pertain to the framework employed by the coroner (4.15). Furthermore, we do not believe that drug dependence per se can ever be a cause of death, and we doubt whether drug psychosis is a feasible cause of death.

4.25   Further complications arise from the way in which the five main three-digit ICD9 codes are subdivided into more specific four-digit codes. These four-digit codes mostly cover groups of drugs, and therefore cannot be used to derive the number of deaths from specific substances. Moreover, the subcategories are different within the main three-digit code groups so they cannot be added together to give the number of deaths from particular types or groups of drugs. We cannot see this as helpful.

4.26   The four-digit codes cover a broad range of legal and illegal substances, including some that would not be classified as drugs under most conventional definitions. In particular, ICD9 305.0 and ICD9 305.1, which account for a high proportion of deaths coded to ICD9 305, cover non-dependent abuse of alcohol and tobacco, and ICD9 E950.6-9 and E980.6-9 cover 'Agricultural and horticultural chemical and pharmaceutical preparations, other than plant foods or fertilisers'; 'corrosive and caustic substances'; 'arsenic and its compounds'; and 'other and unspecified solid and liquid substances'. Similarly, the majority of deaths coded to ICD9 304.6 are due to volatile substance abuse (VSA). Between 1993 and 1996 around one fifth of deaths attributed to drug dependence (ICD9 304) were coded to ICD9 304.6. It is worth noting that cocaine is coded to 'local anaesthetic' (ICD9 E855.2) under accidental poisoning, but to 'cocaine' under the dependence and abuse codes (ICD9 304.2 and ICD9 305.6). What one is of course looking for is a ready method of using these codes in a way to capture deaths due to any and all substances relevant to the interests of this report, with other chemicals and drugs e.g. weed killer and paracetamol, excluded.

4.27   ONS's current approach to the definition of drug-related deaths (Table 6.1) does not meet the inclusion/exclusion requirements in a way to reflect our needs, and is likely to be considerably over-inclusive from our perspective. Even the restrictive group of codings with which ONS kindly ran certain calculations for the purposes of this report, seem to us potentially over-inclusive in some ways and under-inclusive in others.

4.28   Where a number of drugs are mentioned on a death certificate, it is not always possible to tell which of them made a major contribution to the death. Therefore, ONS's estimates of the number of deaths due to specific drugs are based on the number of deaths where the underlying cause of death was drug-related (i.e. assigned one of the ICD9 codes in Box 4), and where the drug is mentioned on the death certificate. This procedure cannot reveal whether the stated drug was primarily responsible for the death.

4.29   When analysing figures on deaths due to specific drugs, it is important to be aware of these limitations. ONS has recently developed a database which will allow deaths from specific drugs to be extracted more easily and reliably. The database contains all deaths assigned one of the underlying causes of death within ONS's broad definition of drug-related deaths in Box 4. Information for 1993 onwards has been entered onto the database in such a way that ONS can now run queries to retrieve information on the number of cases where particular substances were mentioned on the death certificate, much more efficiently than before. Most of the variables on the death certificate, including age, sex, postcode, occupation and martial status, are stored on the database, and it can therefore be used to carry out much more detailed analysis than was previously feasible.

4.30   ICD10 will be adopted by GRO (Scotland) in 2000, and by ONS and GRO (Northern Ireland) in 2001[2].

THE CURRENT SYSTEM AND ITS PROBLEMS: SCOTLAND

4.31   In Scotland all suspicious deaths must be referred to a procurator fiscal, and the cause of death is determined by the pathologist. There are no inquests. Occasionally, fatal accident inquiries are held but not usually for drug-related deaths. The procurator fiscal does not give a verdict but instead the 'manner of death' is recorded (accident, suicide, homicide, pending investigation, undetermined, self-inflicted or natural), based on police reports and the findings of the pathologist. The procurator fiscal notifies GRO (Scotland) when changes are required to the cause(s) of death reported at the time of registration, and the register entry is annotated accordingly. In virtually all cases this revised information is used to code the cause of death. GRO (Scotland) is notified by the Crown Office of deaths that were considered to be suicides. All deaths are registered within a few days in Scotland, but this is not the case in England and Wales.

4.32   In 1994, GRO (Scotland) introduced new arrangements for collecting information on drug-related deaths. Forensic pathologists conducting post mortems were asked to pay particular attention to deaths which might be drug-related and to complete questionnaires for these deaths, giving greater detail than is applied on the death certificate. GRO (Scotland) also follows up all deaths of young people where the information on the death certificate is vague or suggests an involvement with drugs. Following the introduction of this system, GRO (Scotland) has published annual figures on drug-related deaths in Scotland. These were first published in 1995 with figures for 1992 to 1994. Data from 1994 are based on the new system of collecting data and provide a baseline against which trends can be measured. In quantifying drug-related deaths, GRO (Scotland) uses a slightly different set of ICD codes from those used in England and Wales.

4.33   The new system for collecting information on drug-related deaths has lead to improved data quality. There has been a decline in the proportion of deaths classified in vaguer categories, both in terms of the type of drug involved and whether the deceased was known or suspected to be drug dependent. There has been a corresponding increase in the proportion of deaths given more specific descriptions and a rise in the total number of drug-related deaths recorded, which may be partly explained by improved data collection. The success of this project was facilitated by the fact that most forensic blood analysis is carried out in four main forensic departments. It has therefore been relatively easy to establish good working relations with these departments and keep track of them (Arrundale and Cole, 1995)[3].

4.34   GRO (Scotland) also assigns supplementary codes to causes of death of particular interest, including drug-related deaths, allowing them to be identified easily from their mortality database. The definition of deaths included as 'drug-related' has however altered over the years, so this information cannot be used on its own to give an indication of long-term trends in drug deaths. From 1988 onwards, individual records of drug-related deaths have been held on spreadsheets with each drug mentioned on the death certificate held in a separate cell, facilitating the quantification of deaths due to specific drugs.

THE CURRENT DATA SYSTEM AND ITS PROBLEMS : NORTHERN IRELAND

4.35   In Northern Ireland, the system of referring deaths to a coroner, who then orders a post mortem and an inquest, is similar to the system operating in England and Wales, although the inquest results in a 'finding' rather than a verdict. Where the information provided on the death certificate is vague (for example, if 'drugs overdose' is stated with no mention of which drugs were involved), GRO (Northern Ireland) will contact the coroner responsible for certifying the death to obtain more detailed information. GRO (NI) do not record the individual drugs implicated in deaths in a database.

VARIATIONS IN PROCEDURES ACROSS THE CONSTITUENT PARTS OF THE UK: SOME GENERAL COMMENTS

4.36   We see it as inevitable with the existing differences between the English Coroner and the Scottish Procurator Fiscal, that there should be some differences in the approaches to collection of data on drug-misuse related deaths. For problems of very common cross-country public health concern, it does however seem to us disadvantageous if data collection systems are allowed to vary in their type of output. We will return to this matter when making our recommendations on improvements to data collection (Chapter 5).

OTHER SOURCES OF INFORMATION ON DRUG-RELATED DEATHS IN THE UK

HOME OFFICE: STATISTICAL BULLETIN OF NOTIFIED ADDICTS

4.37   Until 30 April 1997, the Misuse of Drugs (Notification of and Supply to Addicts) Regulations 1973, required doctors to notify the Chief Medical Officer at the Home Office of any persons considered to be, or suspected of being, addicted to any one of 14 controlled drugs. That system is now defunct and we will not comment on it further. A statistical bulletin published details of the notifications, and also of drug-related deaths. The last bulletin contained information of such deaths for the period up to and including 1995.[4]

ST GEORGE'S HOSPITAL MEDICAL SCHOOL: NATIONAL PROGRAMME ON SUBSTANCE ABUSE DEATHS

4.38   The Department of Addictive Behaviour at St George's Hospital Medical School is currently developing a database of drug abuse deaths in the UK under the National Programme on Substance Abuse Deaths, np-SAD[5]. All coroners in England and Wales and Northern Ireland, together with the procurators fiscal in Scotland, have been invited to complete a standard questionnaire on drug-related deaths. This gives more detailed information than is available from the death certificate, including ethnicity, living arrangements and addict status.

4.39   During the first six months of the study, 35 coroners in England and Wales responded to the questionnaire, reporting a total of 247 drug-related deaths (Ghodse et al, 1998b). This increased to 80 coroners and 491 cases during the second 6 month period[6]. The third report covers 96 coroners' jurisdictions and is based on 695 cases[7].

4.40   The group was grateful for the opportunity to discuss this scheme with Professor Ghodse's colleagues and were impressed by the degree of collaboration they had been able to achieve with coroners. Questions remain as to how complete the coverage obtained would be if the scheme remained open, and the costs of keeping a satisfactory level of collaboration in place in the longer term on this informal basis are unclear.

DEPARTMENT OF THE ENVIRONMENT, TRANSPORT AND THE REGIONS

4.41   The DETR's three-year study into the presence of drugs – medicinal and illegal- in road traffic fatalities (drivers/riders, passengers, cyclists and pedestrians) ended in October 1999 and a full report is expected to be published in Spring 2000. Interim figures released in February 1998 showed a presence of illegal drugs in 16% of the victims and medicinal drugs in 6% – it also showed a presence of alcohol in 34% (23% over the legal limit).[8]

4.42   There are various problems involved in collecting and interpreting these data. For example, cannabis, which is by far the most common illicit drug to be detected in the victims of road traffic accidents, may remain in the body for up to four weeks, and therefore even where it is detected it may not have played a role in an accident (see 2.28). Moreover, the results do not represent comprehensive figures on road traffic accidents due to drugs because only the deceased is tested for the presence of drugs. Where a driver under the influence of drugs causes a fatal accident but survives, this would not be included in the figures of drug-related traffic accidents presented in this study.

4.43   Nevertheless, the results revealed a considerable increase in the proportion of fatalities where drugs were detected in road traffic accident victims compared with a similar study in 1985–87, suggesting there is an increasing need for routine testing for the presence of drugs following road traffic accidents.

COMMUNICABLE DISEASE SURVEILLANCE CENTRE (CDSC)

4.44   Data on HIV/AIDS deaths produced by CDSC and SCIEH, are known to be more comprehensive than those published in routine mortality statistics because HIV/AIDS is not always declared as a cause of death on the death certificate. CDSC receives copies of death certificates mentioning HIV/AIDS from ONS on a monthly basis. They also received reports of HIV/AIDS cases in England and Wales from laboratories and clinicians and they are notified of the deaths of these cases by clinicians, whether or not the cause of death was directly related to HIV/AIDS. The information on risk factors for most of these cases is believed to be fairly accurate.

4.45   The incidence of acute hepatitis B was once a reliable indicator of heroin dependence in the UK but this association is now less firm. Surveillance of hepatitis B and C is less comprehensive than for HIV/AIDS. Cases of acute hepatitis B and chronic hepatitis B and C are received from laboratories, but high completeness of reporting only exists for hepatitis B. Risk factors for hepatitis B cases are often given but there is a substantial proportion of cases for which the risk exposures are unknown. Where an individual has died from hepatitis this may be indicated on the laboratory reports but this is not necessarily the case. Comprehensive information on risk factors among individuals dying from hepatitis B is therefore not available.

4.46   In the case of hepatitis C, most reported infections are found by screening risk groups. CDSC are establishing surveillance of end-stage liver disease due to hepatitis B and C which will incorporate deaths, although this will not be comprehensive for the whole country owing to lack of funding. Data on how hepatitis C was acquired is requested but is missing in a high proportion of cases.

4.47   We return later to this worrying incompleteness in data reporting on drug-related hepatitis deaths, and this is certainly a further problem that needs to be flagged up.

INTERNATIONAL DATA

4.48   There have been various developments at an international level to improve the quality and comparability of statistics on drug-related deaths. At the European level, two major studies have been commissioned by the European Monitoring Centre for Drugs and Drug Addiction (EMCDDA) in recent years. The first of these was co-ordinated by the National Board of Health in Denmark[9], and the second by the Trimbos Institute (the Netherlands Institute of Mental Health and Addiction) (van Laar and de Zwart, 1998). These studies have confirmed that there is considerable variation between countries in methods of collecting, recording, coding and quantifying information on drug-related deaths.

4.49   One of the key outcomes from these studies is the development of a draft standard set of criteria, for extracting data on drug-related deaths from general mortality registers and from special registers, 'the DRD-Standard' (EMCDDA, 1999)[10]. The feasibility of implementing this standard in EU member states has been assessed by the Trimbos Institute on behalf of the EMCDDA, based on information collected via a questionnaire to each country (EMCDDA 1999). The second stage of this exercise will be to collect data according to these codes from member states and analyse them. We refer in Chapter 6 to analysis of British data conducted within the DRD system.

DATA SYSTEM ON DRUG MISUSE : CONCLUSION

4.50   We conclude that the current system for collecting and reporting on drug-related deaths in the UK stands in need of considerable strengthening, particularly so in England, Wales and Northern Ireland. However, such a judgement should not be seen as negative. In working toward the needed improvements there is valuable experience on which to build. The Coroner's Courts and the Procurator Fiscal system represent a remarkably strong, experienced and community based device which although constituted with other formal responsibilities, is already giving considerable support to public health interests. The Government statistical offices have given a great deal of thought to data collection in this area and are cognisant of the problems. Potentially valuable international collaboration is developing. But the fact remains that at present the system for generating data on drug-related deaths cannot provide information of the quality needed.

5 IMPROVING THE DATA BASE

In Chapter 4 we identified the current problems within the system for generating data on drug-related deaths. In this chapter we consider how these problems can be met, one by one. The summed intention is, however, to make radical proposals for strengthening the overall system, so that its output can support prevention of drug-related deaths.

THE PROBLEM

5.1 What is apparent from Chapter 4 and what has become increasingly apparent as we have undertaken this enquiry, has been the lack of reliability of the data on drug-related deaths. That is not to say that the data which are collected have no value. Indeed it seems to be possible, as is shown by Chapter 6, to draw some conclusions from them essentially in terms of trends over time. However, the data are not good in identifying actual numbers of drug-related deaths and, in order that real faith can be put in them, they need to be improved.

5.2 Good policy formulation requires good underpinning information, and at the moment that it is not the situation for drug-related deaths. The UK Anti-Drugs Co-ordinator's first annual report and national plan (published May 1999)[1], has as one of its performance indicators the reduction of drug-related deaths and it is obviously important that such an indicator should be soundly based.

5.3 The ability of ONS to classify a death as drug-related depends upon the information which is available to them. At the moment it is often poor or missing. The question is how that information is to be improved. In an ideal world all deaths where drugs were in some way implicated would be identified and recorded systematically. In practice it is unlikely that the ideal can be completely realised, but there is undoubtedly scope for great improvement in the present position.

MAKING IMPROVEMENTS

5.4 In Table 4.1 we listed the problems which currently tend to impair the ability of the system to deliver data of the quality needed for purposes of policy. In the section which follows, we will deal with those problems point by point and make suggestions as to how they can be met.

5.5 Any proposals for improvement in this system must be workable in practice. Within that perspective:

- It seems to us better to build on the existing system rather than sweep it away and propose something entirely new.

- Any suggestions we make will be parsimonious in that we will only ask for additional data to be collected when they are of clear relevance to policy needs.

- Cost implications will be borne in mind, but we believe that some extra investment is needed.

- In that the system will continue to rely on the conjoint actions of several different categories of professionals, we see it as necessary that our proposals should be sensitive to their working lives and statutory responsibilities, and we say this particularly in relation to the role of coroners.

- There are also public implications which need to be handled sensitively in relation to the possible impact of any proposals on the feelings of bereaved relatives and friends.

5.6   In that any improvements in data collection will be likely to distort the present system and bear on the interpretation of trends, there will be advantage in instituting one new system over a relatively short term rather than going for a spaced series of revisions.

DATA ON DEATHS DUE TO VIRUS-RELATED CHRONIC ILLNESS

5.7   As we noted in 4.9, drug-related deaths due to chronic virus diseases are not likely to be adequately captured in the system, and we see no way at present in which a coroner could be expected reliably to identify these deaths.

5.8   Given the large and evidently growing number of people with hepatitis C infection, we think it is essential that a system is put in place for monitoring trends in hepatitis C related liver disease and related mortality. We recommend that a national surveillance system is developed, analogous to that for the voluntary reporting of AIDS cases, involving hospital consultants responsible for managing patients with chronic hepatitis, cirrhosis and liver cancer. Such patients should already be tested for their hepatitis B and hepatitis C status. Those testing positive should be asked about possible risk factors, including previous injecting drug use, and blood or blood product transfusion. This information should then be recorded on a standardised form along with the patient's gender, date of birth, place of residence and country of origin and sent for analysis at national centres such as the Communicable Disease Surveillance Centre and the Scottish Centre for Infection and Environmental Health. The data could then be linked to the death registers to ascertain mortality rates.

5.9   We further believe that it is also necessary to monitor more systematically the trends in hepatitis C infection rates among injecting drug users throughout the country. Without such data, the country will be unaware of the true extent of this major challenge to individual and public health. We thus recommend that on a regular two-yearly basis, anonymised salivary hepatitis C testing should be conducted on a representative sample of drug projects and drug dependency treatment units, across the country. A standardised anonymised form should be completed over, say, a two-month period for all new attenders reporting current or recent injecting. It should record the individual's gender, date of birth, area of residence and year when started injecting. A national centre would then collect, analyse and report upon the data.

THE RESPONSIBILITY OF CORONERS

5.10   What we say in the following section relates only to England and Wales and with minor adjustment to Northern Ireland: Scotland is considered separately later. We have remarked on several difficulties in relation to the completeness and meaningfulness for public health purposes of data currently collected by coroners (4.11, 4.12, 4.15, 4.18). If the current Certificate (Appendix 1) was revised to give a structured format for recording information on drug-related deaths, we believe that this would be very helpful. However, we strongly recommend that in the actualisation of any suggestions which bear on the work of coroners, the Coroners Society of England and Wales should be fully consulted. It would be a great mistake for any arrangements to be imposed on coroners without their agreement. At a local level Directors of Public Health could have an important liaison role with coroners.

THE CORONER AND USE OF FORENSIC TOXICOLOGICAL EXAMINATIONS

5.11   Identification of any drug implication in a death will depend to a large extent on whether post mortems are carried out, and whether they include a toxicological examination. In England and Wales whether a post mortem includes a toxicological examination is dependent on whether the coroner (perhaps on the advice of the pathologist), judges one is necessary to determine the medical cause of death. We think there may be inconsistencies, and in some cases we understand that the decision may be influenced by resource constraints. In Scotland toxicology examinations are routinely undertaken at post mortem.

5.12   Of the 195,000 deaths which are referred to coroners, 70% are aged over 65. Furthermore, about 70,000 deaths are found to be from natural causes without resort to post mortems. About 125,000 cases go to post mortem, and that would appear to be the point at which any drug implications should be confirmed or identified. We do not know what proportion of those post mortems routinely involve a toxicological examination, or what the additional costs of routinely requiring such examinations would be.

5.13   The most radical solution would be for all 125,000 post mortems to involve a toxicological screening (followed if necessary by closer examination), for controlled drugs. Mandatory testing and the wait for the pathologist's report might slow the work of the Coroners Office in an unwelcome way. There may be difficulties in terms of cost or propriety (under the Human Tissues Act 1961), if there is no reason to believe that drugs were causally implicated. We think therefore that judgement should be made on the basis of the considerations in the next paragraph.

5.14   We strongly recommend that toxicological screening and examination should be ordered by the coroner where he or she has reason to believe that controlled drugs were implicated. The threshold for this decision should be low. In addition, in any person aged between 15 and 50 where the cause of death is not evident, drug screening should be conducted. Where there are resource implications in any particular areas even for this restricted degree of toxicological screening and examination, these should be overcome with the assistance of Local Authorities.

RECORDING OF RELEVANT INFORMA

5.15   The choice of verdicts at present   ory
       (4.16). For the reasons stated, we   ug-
       related categories, leaving:

              Accident/misadventure

              Suicide

              Lawful killing

              Unlawful killing

              Open

5.16   We suggest that Part V of the Cor   then
       invite recording of any relevant i   tance
       misuse in the death. We would e   with
       the Coroners' Society before being   rhaps
       to the right of the page), set out ir

              (i) Controlled drugs, alcoh   part
                 cause of this death Yes/

       (ii) If "yes" list all substances and underline those principally involved.

       (iii) Was injected drug misuse causally involved? Yes/No

       (iv) Was toxicology employed? Yes/No

5.17   We believe that, in principle, the suggestion that information of the kind we propose does not go beyond the sort of statistical data already recorded on the coroner's certificate in other circumstances, although this may go beyond what the coroner is required by law to do.

5.18   We would not want to see the coroner's unstructured recording on "time place and circumstances", squeezed out by the proposals made in 5.16.

5.19   Significant resource implications would in our view not arise in relation to the actual recording of answers to the questions put in 5.17. However, the demands on occasion of slightly wider background enquiries, might have resource implications. If that is the case, we believe that a way should be found to meet the extra support needed.

5.20   We are aware that the Coroners' Society already has in place a useful series of training events. There would be advantage if training events could be offered regularly on the coroner's work regarding drug-related deaths. Indeed, we see that kind of training input as vital in building the informed support of the kinds we are proposing and in ensuring uniformity of practice. We ask that copies of this present ACMD report are made available to all coroners.

SCOTLAND AND THE ROLE OF THE PROCURATOR FISCAL

5.21   The role of the Procurator Fiscal is in several ways different from that of the coroner, and we are aware that in Scotland efforts have over recent years already been made to strengthen reporting on drug-related deaths. We believe, however that the suggestions for a new format for recording information on drug-related deaths (4.23 and 4.24) should also be implemented in Scotland, and would again hope that copies of the present report could be made available to all procurators fiscal.

THE ROLE OF ONS IN STRENGTHENING THE DATA COLLECTION

5.22   The proposals we make above in relation to the role of the coroner and procurator fiscal, will have a direct and beneficial impact on the ability of ONS to collect more detailed and reliable data on drug-related deaths.

5.23   We do however believe that questions around how best to group the ICD codings so as to give the most meaningful overall count of "drug-related deaths", still need to be sorted out. The present standard ONS approach is for our purposes unsatisfactory, and we are concerned that ONS and GRO (Scotland) are employing different coding rules. We note that ICD10 will be adopted by GRO(S) in 2000 and by ONS and GRO (NI) in 2001. The matters involved are complex and we do not believe that we should go to a detailed level in this report. However, we suggest that a short-life technical working group should be brought together under an agreed lead, to reach a UK-wide agreement on an approach which could be expected to serve the relevant national policy needs over the next ten years at least. We suspect that DOH, Health Departments, the UK Anti-Drugs Co-ordination Unit and ACMD, would want to have representation on such a group, as well as the statistical offices.

5.24   It seems to us unsatisfactory that ONS does not have a formal way of checking back when needed with the Coroner's Office (4.22). We suggest that this should be remedied. We note that medical enquiries may be re-instituted in 2001.

DATA ON DRUG MISUSE DEATHS AND ROAD TRAFFIC ACCIDENTS

5.25   Understanding of issues around this important topic is still at a stage of development. We would like to encourage further research and development, but have no specific recommendations to make.

INTERNATIONAL COMPARISONS

5.26   We have earlier stated our view that the basis for international comparisons on drug-related deaths is not at present reliable (4.48). Such work does however deserve support. We were pleased to note that the UK is involved in international collaboration exercises, and believe that such works deserve continuing support.

IMPROVING THE DATA BASE: CONCLUSIONS

5.27   Our review of the issues involved persuades us that, building on the present system, there are a number of evident and feasible separate ways in which data-collection on drug-related deaths can be significantly improved. The aim must be to get a total system working better. The result will then be a greatly improved data base to inform and strengthen policies on prevention of drug-related deaths both at national and at local level. We strongly recommend that the necessary consultations to help set up this new overall system are quickly got underway, with the needed resources to support the establishment of the system then duly found. In our view the country's response to the problem set by deaths due to drug misuse will be grossly handicapped unless and until the recommendations made here are met.

6 DRUG-RELATED DEATHS: SOME KEY OUTPUT FROM THE PRESENTLY AVAILABLE DATA SOURCES

We present here some key data on the incidence of drug-related deaths in this country, and trends over time. That there has been a profound worsening over the last 10 years or so, cannot be doubted

LOOKING FOR THE MOST MEANINGFUL CATEGORISATION

6.1 As mentioned earlier (4.29) we believe that the ONS approach, whether in terms of their usual reporting or the analysis kindly made available to us for purposes of this report, may include in the tallies too many deaths which are not drug-misuse-related and may miss some that are. For the sets of data which are presented here, we will rely on two sources. First, we will present some overall estimates of drug-misuse deaths which are based on the European Monitoring Centre for Drugs and Drug Addiction (EMCDDA) group categorisation of drug misuse deaths, and which is more restrictive than the standard ONS approach. Second, we present data which were prepared for us by ONS on the basis of a more restricted approach than the standard ONS way of reporting drug-related deaths. Table 6.1 gives details on the ICD9 (ninth revision of WHO's International Classifications of Diseases) contained in each of 3 approaches: EMCDDA's DRD standard, the restricted ONS approach, and the standard ONS approach. For practical purposes the situation may be summarised by saying that EMCDDA, ONS standard and ONS restricted, are rank ordered in terms of stricter as opposed to broader definition. We doubt whether any of their systems can be recommended as the universal solution, but do not see this as the place for their fine-grained dissection.

Table 6.1 ICD 9 codes contained within each of 3 systems that may be employed to represent acute deaths due to drug misuse.

SYSTEM	ICD9 CODE NUMBERS	MEANING OF CODE
EMCDDA	292	Drug psychosis
	304	Drug dependence
	305 2–9	Non-dependent abuse of drugs
	E850.0	Accidental poisoning – opiates and related narcotics
	E854.1	Accidental poisoning – psychodysleptics (hallucinogens)
	E854.2	Accidental poisoning – psychostimulants
ONS restricted	304	As above
	305 2–9	As above
	965.0	Poisoning by opiates and related narcotics
	967	Poisoning by sedatives and hypnotics
	968.5	Poisoning by surface and infiltration anaesthetics (including cocaine)
	969	Poisoning by psychotropic agents
	977 8–9	Poisoning by other and unspecified drugs and medicaments.
ONS standard	292	As above
	304	As above
	305 2–9	As above
	E850–E858	Accidental poisoning by drugs, medicaments and biologicals
	E950.0–5	Suicide and self-inflicted poisoning by solid or liquid substances, drugs and medicaments
	E962.0	Assault by poisoning – drugs and medicaments

ACUTE DRUG-RELATED MORTALITY IN ENGLAND AND WALES BASED ON THE EMCDDA DEFINITION

6.2   Figure 6.1 provides a graphic presentation separately of male and female drug-related mortality in England and Wales, for the years 1979 to 1997. The vertical axis represents age-standardised rates of death per million living. In Table 6.2, rather than giving rates per million, we tabulate the actual number of deaths for each year. We believe these figures represent the best available approximation to the acute drug-related deaths occurring over this period as a result of accidental overdose among drug misusers. They exclude some combinations of drugs coded to external causes e.g.

ICD 9 850.8 and 850.9, and 850.0.

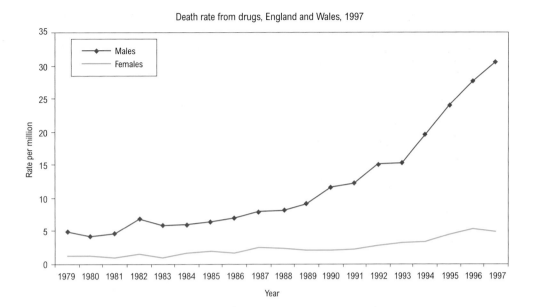

Figure 6.1 Age standardised mortality rate from drugs where the underlying cause of death was : ICD9 292, 304, 305.2–9, E850.0, E854.1–2, England and Wales, 1979–1997. These figures are based on the EMCDDA definition.

Table 6.2 Number of deaths where the underlying cause was ICD9 292, 304, 305.2–9, E850.0, E854.1–2. (EMCDDA approach) England and Wales 1979–1998

	Males	Females	Total	Male:Female Ratio
1979	122	30	152	4.07
1980	106	32	138	3.31
1981	117	26	143	4.50
1982	177	37	214	4.78
1983	153	25	178	6.12
1984	158	42	200	3.76
1985	170	51	221	3.33
1986	188	44	232	4.27
1987	219	70	289	3.13
1988	213	62	275	3.44
1989	244	54	298	4.52
1990	309	54	363	5.72
1991	325	59	384	5.51
1992	403	74	477	5.45
1993	410	83	493	4.94
1994	526	86	612	6.12
1995	646	115	761	5.62
1996	748	141	889	5.30
1997	820	124	944	6.61
1998	888	188	1076	4.72

6.3   From Figure 6.1 and Table 6.1 the following conclusions can be drawn.

• From about 1980 onwards, slowly at first and then more steeply, deaths related to drug misuse increased very significantly for men, and significantly but less steeply and from a lower base, for women

• At the beginning of this period the male/female death ratio was 4.5:1 while at the end of the period the ratio had increased to 6.6:1.

• We suspect but cannot prove that for both sexes, the increase in acute deaths was to a significant degree causally related to an increased incidence of injecting drug misuse.

• It is likely that the observed male/female ratios in part reflect underlying differentials in prevalence of drug misuse, but we cannot rule out the influence of gender-related contextual factors.

• Our overall conclusion is that at a conservative estimate the number of people in England and Wales dying immediately as a result of drug misuse in 1998 was 888 for men and 188 for women, or in total 1076. This figure excludes suicides by drug users. The restricted ONS approach would give figures of 1589 and 661 (total 2250) while the standard ONS approach gives 1944 for men and 928 for women (total 2922).

AGE AND "ACCIDENTAL" DEATHS DUE TO DRUG MISUSE

6.4   ONS suggests that their restricted tabulations of drug-related deaths, when limited to the "accidents" heading as opposed to "suicide" or "undetermined" headings, are likely to reflect trends in drug misuse deaths. We present such data in Fig. 6.2 for England and Wales, not as representing absolute numbers, but as a fair reflection of trends in acute drug-related deaths by age. This figure deals with male deaths only, because the total deaths among females were not in a range meaningfully to allow break down by age group. For male mortality by age, we conclude:

• For the greater part of the period 1979–1997, it was the age group 20–29 which was most at risk.

• In the 1990s it was the 20–29 age group which showed the most dramatic acceleration in death rates.

• Rather different temporal points of take-off are seen for different age groups but subjects at all ages under 50 now contribute significantly to the overall "accident" related mortality figures, and all groups within the under 50 band have significantly increased their relevant mortality rates over the stated period. It is worrying to see the 15–19 year group becoming a significant contributor. Our overall conclusion is that the minimum number of people in England and Wales dying immediately as a result of drug misuse in 1998 was 888 for men and 188 for women, or in total 1076. The restricted ONS approach would give figures of 1589 and 661 (total 2250) while the standard ONS approach gives 1944 for men and 928 for women (total 2922). There is good reason, however, to believe that the minimum figures are an under-estimate. First the St George's national programme on substance abuse deaths recorded 1386 deaths in 1998, having received reports from only 56% of coroners in the first six months and 68% in the second. Some coroners may not report a death as substance misuse related, even when the evidence may point to this.

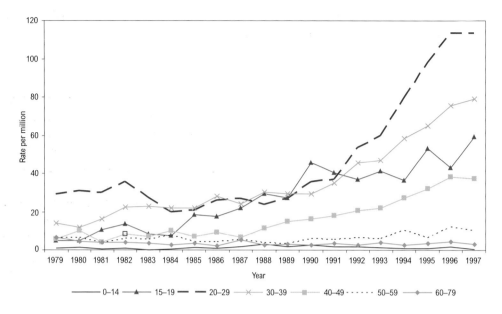

Figure 6.2 Male age specific mortality rates from drugs of abuse, 'Accidents', England and Wales, 1979–1997

YEARS OF LIFE LOST

6.5   Counting the annual number of fatalities is one way of representing the size of the problem. But if comparisons are to be made between the burden of drug-related deaths and those occurring from any other cause, it can be useful also to analyse the data in terms of years of life lost. That latter approach looks at the age to which any individual would have expected to live, if they had not died as a result of their drug use. This is a device which is able to reflect the fact that part of the innate tragedy of drug misuse, is that so many people die young. We have here a measure which can be summed for years of life denied. ONS state that calculations for England and Wales based on their restricted categorisations, suggest that in 1995 drug misuse deaths accounted for 5% of male years of life lost, or 40,550 of years of life lost in comparison to 58,000 from road traffic accidents. The years of life lost through drug misuse are converging with the traffic accident figures as the former goes up and the latter down.

DRUG-RELATED MORTALITY BY GEOGRAPHICAL LOCATION

6.6   Given the many uncertainties in the system with generates these data and in particular the possible variation in reporting practice between different coroners (4.13), we caution against putting too great faith in current mapping of drug-related deaths by place of residence of the deceased. We, note, however that techniques are in principle available to ONS which allow the pinpointing of residential areas which are experiencing a high drug misuse mortality, down to the level of say, particular housing estates.

DRUG-RELATED MORTALITY BY SOCIAL DEPRIVATION

6.7   ONS have made available to us (Fig 6.3) a graph expressing the relation between age standardised mortality rates for the "accident" drug-related deaths (restricted approach), and the Carstairs deprivation scores relating to place of usual residence of the deceased. Data have been grouped across the years 1991–1997. We interpret this figure as indicating for men and especially for young men, a strong positive relationship between deprivation and incidence of drug-related deaths by "accident". Among men aged 15–44, deaths among subject in the 5th (extreme) quintile of deprivation, were over these years 6 times that seen in the least deprived. We are unable to say how far these deprivation-related differentials among men reflect corresponding prevalence rates of drugs misuse, as opposed to contextual factors such as pattern of use, circumstances of overdose or access to emergency help.

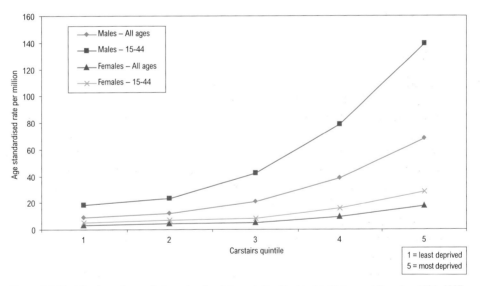

Figure 6.3 Mortality from drugs of abuse by Carstairs quintile, 'Accidents', Males and Females 1991–1997

6.8   The figure shows a relationship between deprivation and "accident" drug-related mortality for women but the trend is not so marked as among men and the age differences are not so prominent.

6.9   We referred earlier to some research data on the relationship between deprivation and drug-related deaths and would at this point like to draw attention again to the Scottish data given in paragraph 3.10.

DEATHS BY DRUG TYPE

6.10   Data are available, by year, on how often selected drugs are mentioned on death certificates. We have thought it useful to make some use of this data in Chapter 7, when comparing trends where methadone and other opioids are stated to be involved. What stands out with total clarity is that year after year it is heroin misuse which is making the major contribution to drug-related deaths. Otherwise, we suspect that these data are at present not very interpretable (4.18), especially so where small numbers are involved as with cocaine, ecstasy and amphetamines. From 1993 to 1997 there was a decrease from 354 to 221 in temazepam "mentions" and an increase from 129 to 289 in mentions of diazepam, but in our view the interpretation of these findings is uncertain.

DRUG-RELATED DEATHS IN SCOTLAND

6.11   As we have already mentioned (para 4.31) the GRO (Scotland) has been reporting on drug-related deaths since 1992 and has used an enhanced system since 1994. Figure 6.4 shows that both all drug-related deaths and those of persons known or suspected to be drug dependent, have not risen greatly since 1994, peaking at 55 per million and at 36 per million population respectively in 1998.

6.12   Since 1996, the GRO (Scotland) has been reporting on the drugs detected in the deceased. These are shown in Table 6.3. Of particular note are the large number of cases involving benzodiazepines and the reduction in number of methadone "mentions" from 91 in 1996 to 64 in 1998. Over the same period heroin "mentions" increased from 82 to 114.

Source: General Register Office for Scotland, 1999

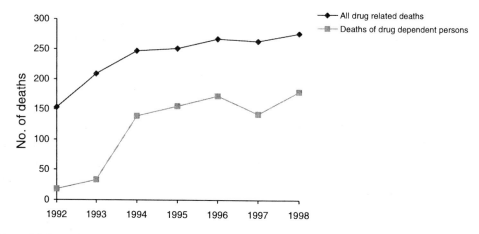

Figure 6.4 Drug-related deaths in Scotland 1992-98

Table 6.3 Drugs mentioned on the pathologist's form for drug-related deaths in Scotland 1996–98. Note that more than one drug may have been mentioned in relation to a single death.

	1996	1997	1998
Heroin/morphine	82	80	114
Diazepam	72	69	105
Temazepam	37	25	46
Methadone	91	79	64
Other	10	6	7
Total	212	259	336

DRUG-RELATED DEATHS IN NORTHERN IRELAND

6.13   There are comparatively few drug-related deaths in Northern Ireland. Levels remain fairly consistent over time.

CONCLUSIONS

6.14   The data which we are able to present in this chapter between them fall far short of constituting the kind of reliable and comprehensive picture of trends and situations which are needed to support informed national and local policies on prevention of drug-related deaths. We believe, however, that there is nothing but advantage in displaying and admitting these difficulties and no blame attaches to any individual or institution. But it is not a happy state of affairs that on such a core statistic as the number of deaths due to drug-misuse in England and Wales in 1998 the estimates vary about three-fold (1076–2922), according to the approach employed. Our strong recommendation is inevitably therefore that attention needs to be given to a radical strengthening of the data system.

6.15   Despite these difficulties we believe that some reasonably confident conclusions can be drawn from the data presented here. From about 1980 onwards, drug-related deaths in England and Wales have been increasing and in 1998 were at almost 8 times the 1980 level (we put more confidence in the trend than in the absolute figures). In Scotland the upward trend seems to have levelled out. Many more men are dying than women (a 6.6 fold ratio). It is the age group 20–29 which has recently shown the steepest rise in drug-related deaths and the burden of years of life lost is heavy. Drug-related deaths are strongly related to social deprivation. Heroin continues to be the drug which is predominantly involved, methadone is of substantial significance, and benzodiazepines make a contribution.

6.16   In summary, we conclude that the data which are available provide a useful characterisation of some aspects of the situation and more confidently of trends.

At the same time they point up the gaps and uncertainties, and emphasise the need for a much strengthened data system.

7 METHADONE

Methadone is a valuable drug in the treatment of opioid dependence. But it is two-edged in that if carelessly employed it can add to the toll of opioid-related deaths.

INTRODUCTION

7.1 Methadone is by far the most widely prescribed drug in the treatment of opioid dependence. In England and Wales in 1995 there were estimated to be about 30,000 people receiving methadone treatment of one type or another from community pharmacies[1]. However, in recent years methadone has been associated with large numbers of drug-related deaths. In England and Wales the reported number rose from 371 in 1993 to 674 in 1997 (Table 7.1). The trend in Scotland is more encouraging with methadone-related cases falling from 91 in 1996 to 64 in 1998. The possible reasons for the fall in Scotland will be considered in para 7.20.

7.2 In writing this chapter we have been greatly assisted by Professor Wayne Hall, of the National Drug and Alcohol Research Centre, New South Wales, Australia, who undertook for us a review of trends in methadone-related deaths in the UK 1985–1995[2]. We have also been greatly assisted by the Department of Health's recently published guidelines on clinical management of drug misuse[3]. This chapter provides practical and detailed advice as to how the prescription of methadone to drug users should be handled, in ways which will increase benefit and decrease associated risks. This advice is relevant to the individual doctors and pharmacists who may be concerned, but it also has a bearing on institutional policies.

Table 7.1 Deaths where methadone was mentioned on the death certificate, alone or in combination, England and Wales; data supplied by ONS using their 'standard' definition.

	Methadone (all mentions)	Methadone in combination with other drugs	Methadone in combination with alcohol
1993 (Provisional *)	230	92	49
1994	269	110	57
1995	310	130	58
1996	368	141	87
1997	421	152	102

* Additional details on the circumstances of a death may be recorded in Part V of the coroner's certificate for some deaths. For completeness, substances mentioned in this section were included on the new ONS drugs database. At present, for 1993 the text in Part V has only been entered onto the ONS mortality database for around half the deaths for this year (1993). Until the remaining text for 1993 has been entered, figures for that year are provisional.

7.3   A recent increase in concern over the contribution that methadone may be making to the count of opioid deaths is not restricted to this country[4-9]. This issue has for instance, recently attracted a lot of attention in Australia[10-13], the USA[14-18] and in European countries.

METHADONE : MODE OF USE AND THERAPEUTIC BENEFITS

7.4   Methadone is used either to help people withdraw from opioid use or to maintain them on the drug, usually taken orally in the form of methadone mixture (Martindale 1999)[19], as a replacement for the opioid on which they have been relying. The intention of maintenance is to prevent withdrawal symptoms, relieve drug hunger and help the patient move away from injecting use. The expectation is that these individuals will then be able to improve their social functioning, and take advantage of wider aspects of treatment and rehabilitation[3].

7.5   In summary, there are four identified benefits of methadone maintenance treatment; a decrease in illicit drug use[20-21]; a reduction of injecting behaviour leading to a decrease in viral transmission[22-32]; a reduction in the risk of opioid overdose death of those in treatment[12 and 33-35]; and a decrease in criminal activity[36-38]. We believe that there is strong and multiple support in the research literature for such gains when methadone is given in adequate dosage, with consistency, with adequate supervision and in the context of psycho-social support.

7.6   In Britain any medical practitioner can, at present, prescribe methadone for opioid dependence: patients usually consume their methadone at home rather than under direct clinical supervision and one third of all prescriptions are, at present, for a weekly or fortnightly pick-up. Compared to other countries there is minimal central regulation of methadone maintenance treatment, and prescribing practice is not uniform although there are guidelines in existence. As a result, it is not always clear whether GP prescribing is for maintenance or extended withdrawal.

PHARMACOLOGY AND TOXICOLOGY

7.7   Without going into the pharmacology and toxicology of methadone it is sufficient for us to note that there are large differences between individuals in the accumulation and clearance of the drug in the body[39]. A fatal dose for a naïve or non-tolerant individual, might be the same (or less) than the daily dose of a person in methadone maintenance treatment. In general, methadone has a fairly narrow window of safety. The difference between the dose needed for effective maintenance and the dose which will kill an individual, is small.

FACTORS INFLUENCING PREVALENCE OF METHADONE-RELATED DEATHS

INCREASED PREVALENCE OF METHADONE PRESCRIBING

7.8   In considering what factors contribute to the prevalence of methadone-related deaths it can be concluded that the increased availability of methadone maintenance treatment with weak or absent controls on supervision of methadone, is a risk factor for overdose deaths involving diverted methadone. Those enrolled in methadone maintenance treatment programmes are much less likely to die from methadone overdose than those not enrolled (although the risk is greater at induction of maintenance treatment). It follows that increased restriction on take-away prescribing of methadone might decrease the risk of methadone-related deaths.

7.9   An increase in methadone-related deaths may also reflect the fact that more people are receiving the treatment. It could be argued that with a risk attaching to methadone maintenance, a desirable expansion of service provision will therefore result in an inevitable increase in methadone-related deaths as the downside. We do not ourselves accept the concept here of fixed risk or inevitability.

7.10   It could be argued that there may be an inverse relationship between the number of heroin and methadone-related deaths, with reductions in heroin overdose deaths partially offset by an increase in methadone-related overdose deaths. If this is true then the answer should be to find a system which does not lose the benefit of reducing heroin-related deaths by increasing methadone-related deaths, but which has appropriate prescribing controls built in, so as to obviate the downside.

METHADONE AND INTERACTION WITH ALCOHOL AND OTHER DRUGS

7.11   A dose of methadone which would not, in itself, be likely to be dangerous can be fatal if taken in combination with other drugs. Opioids, benzodiazepines and alcohol are the drugs most likely to give rise to these kinds of combined fatalities[40–45] and Table 7.1 gives some indication of the commonness of such events. It is our impression that users themselves are not adequately aware of these dangers, and prescribers and other drugs agency workers are not always properly cautious. A useful listing of drug interactions with methadone is given as Annex 4 to the Guidelines[3].

DEATHS BY ACCIDENTAL POISONING

7.12   Careless home storage occasionally results in a child dying as a result of swallowing an adult's prescribed methadone. This can be avoided if the methadone is consumed by the patient under supervision. Whenever methadone is dispensed for home consumption, clinic staff, GPs and pharmacists, should advise the patient on the need for safe storage. Clear hazard warnings on the bottle can help reinforce the message.

METHADONE: OPTIMISING CLINICAL USEFULNESS WHILE REDUCING THE RISKS OF OVERDOSE

THE VERY STRONG NEED TO PREVENT METHADONE DIVERSION

7.13   We believe that in the treatment of opioid dependence the benefits which can accrue from the use of methadone treatment if competently delivered, considerably outweigh the disadvantages. The question that needs to be addressed is how to optimise those benefits, while decreasing the disadvantages of deaths caused by methadone poisoning.

7.14   We would not advocate putting such strict and inflexible prescribing controls in place so as to deter a great many opioid users from enrolling in treatment, or from maintaining treatment contact. The unwanted side effect would be that of encouraging continuance of the highly dangerous intravenous use of illicit drugs. While decreasing the risks of methadone diversion, such measures might increase risks to individuals by their exclusion from an effective treatment which saves lives.

7.15   With the need for policies which have within them the capacity for flexibility and response to the individual patient admitted, we believe that over recent years the agency approaches to prescribing and dispensing of methadone have often been too lax. Without throwing away what has been learned and with the need for a continued emphasis on harm minimisation acknowledged, it is our unambiguous conclusion that methadone prescribing should, in future, be conducted in a way which puts more emphasis on preventing diversion. Without that kind of re-positioning, there will be no hope of reducing the significant number of drug deaths which are currently methadone-related.

RECOMMENDATIONS RELATING TO THE PRESCRIBING OF METHADONE

7.16   We fully support the recommendations on methadone prescribing made in the recently revised Guidelines[3]. It would be unnecessary to repeat all those recommendations in the present report, and we will not attempt to go to that level of clinical detail. The recommendations which we now make are, however, compatible with the Guidelines, while also supporting certain administrative proposals which we believe Government is now considering in relation to licensing of doctors to prescribe methadone in the treatment of dependence.

- Induction into methadone is a potentially dangerous process and should be undertaken by doctors who are appropriately trained and experienced. Arrangements should be in place to guarantee such provisions.

- The same expectations and safeguards should apply to the use of the drug for maintenance.

- In our view the normal practice should be for methadone to be taken under daily supervision for at least 6 months and often longer. That expectation should be varied only exceptionally, and if a strong case can be made out in the individual instance. The bigger the dose of methadone which is being prescribed, the greater will be the need for supervision.

- Agencies as well as individual prescribers and pharmacists, should be alert to the danger of diversion, and they must seek pro-actively to avert this danger. This public responsibility to prevent diversion need not in any way cut across responsibilities for care of the individual.

- When methadone is prescribed by the agency, the prescriber and very importantly also the user, should be alert to the dangers of interaction with other drugs and alcohol, and take steps to avert those dangers.

- We advise absolutely against the prescription of methadone tablets to opioid users because of the potential danger of tablets being ground up and injected. In our view any doctor who despite warnings persists in irresponsible practice, should be reported to the GMC.

- We advise against the prescription of methadone ampoules to opioid users by GPs, and again believe that doctors who persist in such practice despite warnings and advice, should be reported. If these ampoules are to be prescribed by clinics it should only be in exceptional circumstances and under stringent control.

In sum under this heading we want to express our profound alarm about the way in which methadone has over recent years been handled in this country. In our view the correction of this problem should be seen as a matter of the utmost priority. The remedies will involve new training, new commitment, and new institutional safeguards, and repeat review. Mere statements of good intention would constitute an entirely inadequate response to the present situation.

*THE STRONG NEED TO MONITOR AND CURTAIL METHADONE-RELATED
DEATHS*

7.17   We believe that there are inalienable personal responsibilities which lie with the individual prescribing doctor to give all medicines only responsibly. So serious is the public health threat posed by methadone deaths that in our view this problem also requires an institutional level of response. Health Authorities as contributors should monitor the quality and efficacy of methadone prescribing in their areas, and in collaboration with the doctors concerned do everything possible to maximise good and safe practice in these regards.

7.18   With due safeguards in place the further extension of methadone availability is something we recommend as likely to save lives.

7.19   However, as already suggested, the important question is how to maximise the benefits from methadone while reducing the associated deaths. As already stated, in our view, the current national level of methadone-related deaths is entirely unacceptable, even if it in part reflects the increasing number of drug users and the increasing number receiving methadone. If allowed to continue unchecked, the number of methadone-related deaths will threaten to discredit an otherwise good treatment. We recommend that deaths from methadone should be closely monitored both locally and nationally. Reduction by an agreed percentage for deaths in which methadone is mentioned as a cause should be a performance indicator as a sub-target within any overall indicator. We are aware that improved data collection systems are likely to increase the number of reports for methadone-related deaths and this must in the short-term bear on the interpretability of any observed trend.

THE SCOTTISH EXPERIENCE WITH METHADONE

7.20   Data from Glasgow show that between 1992 and 1998, the number of patients treated with methadone increased 20-fold, from around 140 to 2800.[46] Methadone-related deaths rose from 3 in 1992 to 23 in 1996, falling to 8 in 1997 and 7 in 1998. By relating the numbers of deaths to the annual quantity of methadone prescribed, it can be seen that the methadone-related death rate has fallen gradually from 1992 onwards and particularly between 1996–1997. (Figure 7.1) In the rest of the Strathclyde region surrounding Glasgow, the methadone-related death rate rose steeply from 1992 to 1995, falling thereafter (Figure 7.1). In Glasgow supervised consumption of methadone began in 1992, became health authority policy in 1994, and was very strongly encouraged from 1996 onwards, since when around 90% of prescriptions have been for supervised consumption. In the rest of Strathclyde, there was no supervised consumption until 1996, since when it has been gradually but incompletely introduced. It is also notable that during the period 1996–1998, Greater Glasgow accounted for over 40% of all the methadone prescribed in Scotland but only 24% of the methadone-related deaths (Drug Misuse Statistics Scotland, 1998 bulletin[47]) These data strongly suggest that the supervised consumption of methadone can prevent methadone-related deaths and allow the number of people treated with methadone to be substantially increased without a concomitant increase in methadone-related deaths.

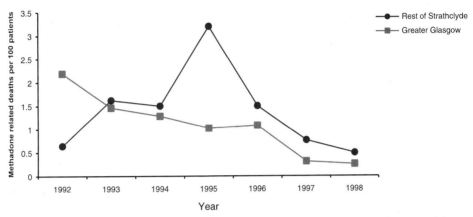

Figure 7.1 Methadone-related death rates per 100 patient years of treatment in Greater Glasgow and the rest of Strathclyde region, 1992-98.

THE NEED FOR RESEARCH ON ALTERNATIVES TO METHADONE

7.21   Methadone is likely, for the foreseeable future, to remain the drug of choice in the maintenance treatment of opioid dependence. We have, however, referred above (7.7) to the inherent disadvantage set by the narrowness of the gap between a safe and a dangerous dose. Clinical evaluations of the utility and safety of drugs such as LAAM (Levo-Alpha-Acetyl Methadol)[48] and buprenorphine[49], does therefore deserve research attention. We do not feel that ACMD has the authority to comment on these issues in detail, but would suggest that in principle there would be considerable public health advantage if an equally effective but safer drug than methadone, could at some time be introduced for medical practice in this arena. That might constitute a significant technological contribution to the prevention of drug-related deaths. We therefore recommend that, as a matter of urgency a Department of Health expert group, should plan and actualise such trials. We hope that financial support would be found from the pharmaceutical industry to support this initiative.

CONCLUSION

7.22   There is incontrovertible evidence for usefulness of methadone in the treatment of opioid dependence, if it is prescribed with due care. However, it is an opioid and in every sense a dangerous drug. When prescribed carelessly it may either kill opioid dependent individuals at induction, or be subject to widespread diversion with risk to illicit market users of death by overdose. The current level of methadone-related deaths is unacceptable. We commend the advice given in the recent Guidelines, and suggest a number of measures which between them should help to reduce these deaths. Patients as well as doctors, pharmacists and agency workers, need to be more aware of the dangers of overdose which can attach to methadone, particularly when used with other substances. There is also a need for much keener awareness of these dangers at institutional and organisational level. We recommend that active steps are taken to ensure such awareness and see DATs as taking a lead role.

8 REDUCING DEATHS FROM THE IMMEDIATE EFFECTS OF TAKING DRUGS

We outline measures which between them will be capable of achieving a very considerable reduction in deaths from the immediate effects of drug taking.

INTRODUCTION

8.1 We have already seen in Chapter 2 that immediate deaths from drug misuse can arise from the direct toxicity of the drug on the heart or respiratory system, from cerebrovascular accidents, and from the effect on other organs. Those are direct effects. They will usually arise from deliberate taking of drugs and occasionally through accidental ingestion. Deaths in which drugs are implicated arise from accidents (to self and others), suicide, homicide, acute infective complications and, rarely, contaminants. That earlier chapter also noted the principal substances involved and the likelihood of the dangers being increased if drugs were taken in combination or with alcohol.

8.2 While death from the immediate effect of taking drugs may not always occur straight away but can take days or weeks, it is convenient to distinguish them from deaths which are not directly attributable to the drugs themselves and are much delayed. The distinction is helpful because of the different policies which can be identified for preventing deaths, depending on the mechanisms by which they occur. Delayed deaths typically arise from virus infections such as HIV and hepatitis B or C transmitted from one injecting drug misuser to another, rather than from the pharmacological and toxicological effects of the drugs, and are the subject of Chapter 9. Some of the issues discussed in Chapter 8 are also of relevance to prevention of deaths from chronic causes. For instance, what we say in this chapter about the prevention of injecting and separately about the need to strengthen care and after-care of drug users who go to prison, is also highly relevant to Chapter 9.

8.3 Given the range of causes of death and of the drugs involved, there is one overarching policy which is likely to help reduce deaths from drug misuse, whether immediate or from chronic disease. That is, a significant reduction in drug misuse itself. We say "likely" rather than certain because it is possible to envisage circumstances where reduction in drug use brought about by swingeingly repressive measures, actually increased risks of death. But ahead of any substantial reduction in the prevalence of misuse, we are convinced that much can be done to reduce the level of deaths. In the remainder of this chapter we consider what, within present realities, can be done to reduce immediate drug-related deaths depending on the drug of misuse and the circumstances which contribute towards death. We will put heavy emphasis on the need to prevent injection of drugs.

PREVENTION OF IMMEDIATE DEATHS WITH A FOCUS ON THE DRUGS

THE DRUGS OF PRIME CONCERN

8.4   As has been seen in Chapter 4, the number of death certificates where opioids (that is, heroin, methadone, morphine, and certain other drugs of this type) were mentioned on the certificate, (see table 4.3), greatly exceeds the number where other drugs were mentioned (963 compared to 313 in 1997). Opioid misuse is therefore a problem deserving of particular attention.

8.5   As discussed in Chapter 7, deaths from methadone have been a cause of considerable concern in recent times. We see reduction in immediate deaths caused by methadone as of vital importance to overall strategies for reduction of immediate drug-related deaths.

8.6   Deaths from opioid misuse in 1997 occurred at a mean age of about 30 (see 6.4) That represents many years of life lost. What is not apparent from the data sources which underlie Chapter 6, is the mode of administration of the drug. However, what has struck us during the course of our enquiry is the extent to which injecting appears to be the predominant route associated with immediate opioid-related deaths, other than for methadone. And injection has of course implications for deaths from chronic disease which are covered in Chapter 9.

8.7   Having stressed the importance of actions targeted at heroin, methadone and other opioids in the prevention of immediate drug-related deaths, the discussion on toxicology given in Chapter 2 makes it clear that preventive action is needed not in relation to just one drug or drug class, but across a wide range of drugs. The focus for special concern may change over time and vary geographically. At present we put up a warning signal about cocaine, see benzodiazepines as making a contribution to the problem, and note the continuing significance of VSA deaths among young people. Furthermore, we would again emphasise that such deaths commonly involve more than one drug taken at the same time, frequently also with alcohol an additional factor. Prevention policies directed at immediate deaths must be based on awareness that the problem is about drugs, about their entrenched or changing popularity and availability and modes of use, and about misuse of drugs taken together purposely or casually, and not simply about any one prime drug or drug type considered in isolation.

LOSS OF TOLERANCE AS AN UNDERLYING DANGER

8.8   Loss of tolerance is frequently implicated in fatal overdose (para 2.12). We recommend that agencies, prescribers and users themselves, should all be made more aware of this risk. The dangers attach both to situations where treatment has led to cessation of opioid use, and to the vulnerability of drug users who have been released from prison. Part of the response in Scotland has been to issue prisoners on release with a credit card sized wallet which provides advice on the dangers of overdosing and mixing drugs, what to do in the event of witnessing an overdose, and where to obtain help. We commend this idea and the same kind of approach might be helpful in treatment agencies.

PREVENTING INJECTED DRUG MISUSE AS A SALIENT ISSUE

8.9   A central conclusion we draw, for preventing both immediate deaths and chronic disease deaths, is the need as a priority to discourage injecting. That is not to say that other forms of harm reduction, such as the supply of sterile needles and syringes, become redundant. Indeed, that work should continue and be strengthened but at the same time we believe that there should be an explicit and complementary emphasis on discouraging injecting. In practical terms, this will mean that those services which see drug misusers should review their policies to ensure that clients who do not currently inject are encouraged **never** to do so. Those who do inject, while being subject to any harm reducing measures connected with their injecting, should be encouraged to cease injecting. Just how that encouragement should be given will depend on the circumstances and the individual, but we believe that services fail in their duty if they do not have policies in place with those aims. Moving people away from injecting is not easy and may not succeed at the first attempt, but confronting this issue should not be ducked. Counselling skills to deal with this problem need to be developed and cognitive – behavioural approaches should be able to assist this kind of behavioural change.

8.10   What we have said in the preceding paragraph has been about people who are probably already deep into a drug taking milieu. At the same time, it is important not to ignore those who are not, or are not yet, part of that culture, and we see a place for getting across a general message about the immediate (and chronic) dangers of injecting. We envisage different forms of message depending on the target audience. The Health Education Authority for England, the appropriate body for Wales, the Health Education Board for Scotland and the Health Promotion Agency in Northern Ireland, should consider the best means of doing so. "Never inject" is a clear and credible message. Everyone involved in drug prevention activity should consider whether they are giving sufficient emphasis to the discouragement of injecting. But we would emphasise strongly that whether the activity is at individual level or targeted at the population, what is needed is information, the building of motivation and support for change, and not the sloganising of scare stories. Again, the matters discussed here are also of great relevance to the prevention of deaths from virus diseases.

THE NEED FOR STRICTER CONTROLS OVER PRESCRIBING

THE PROBLEM IN GENERAL

8.11   There is periodic evidence of levels of prescribing of some drugs which are reckless or, at least, careless and contribute to immediate drug-related deaths. It happens in both NHS and private practice but is worse in private practice[1-4]. The group which produced the Clinical Guidelines[5] for the treatment of drug misuse and dependence recommended to Ministers that a licensing scheme for doctors should be set up which ties in their level of expertise with the types of controlled drugs which they are permitted to give in the treatment of addiction. Any scheme which emerges should, on the one hand, not discourage conscientious doctors from providing treatment for drug dependency yet, on the other, prevents deaths through lax prescribing of controlled drugs or prescribing in an inappropriate form, and which provides a quick means of stopping doctors who prescribe in that way. It is unacceptable that a small number of doctors through poor prescribing practice may contribute causally to drug-related deaths.

8.12   As the scheme is being devised consideration will also need to be given to any problems to which it may give rise, for example, in terms of possible delay in access to treatment.

8.13   Deaths would be reduced if agencies and GPs ceased to prescribe for drug users controlled drugs in tablet form or in ampoules. In our view education, persuasion, and as a final resort disciplinary sanctions, should be deployed to curtail persistent irresponsible practice. (See paragraph 7.16 and our earlier recommendation in relation to methadone.)

BENZODIAZEPINES

8.14   We have already remarked on the high proportion of drug-related deaths in which benzodiazepines are implicated. These statistics suggest to us that there is a need for doctors treating drug misusers, to consider very carefully the appropriateness of their prescribing benzodiazepines. We cannot sufficiently stress that these drugs are both dangerous to drug misusers and easily diverted. We recommend that every agency should have a policy which is sensitive to the needs of individual patients but which will so far as possible avoid prescribing these drugs to new patients, and which will assist current patients to come off them.

8.15   Prescribing benzodiazepines to opioid users (and other drug users), should be seen as exceptional rather than a common clinical decision to be nodded through. We recommend that all agencies critically and urgently review their current level of benzodiazepine prescribing, and in many instances this should lead to very considerable reduction. General practitioners should be advised against prescribing benzodiazepines to drug users without careful assessment of need, and consultation with any agency which may be involved with the patient's care.

8.16   As we noted above (para 7.7), use of benzodiazepines or alcohol or both with opioids, can greatly increase the risk of overdose. There is scope for advising users themselves away from these practices. For services which come into contact with drug users this message should be seen as routine and necessary, with the statement given repeatedly and unambiguously. It is a message which should also be given in the form of more general public health advice.

VOLATILE SUBSTANCE ABUSE (VSA) AS A CONTINUING PROBLEM

8.17   We reported in 1995[6] on volatile substance abuse and suggested, among other things, that efforts should be made to limit the maximum size of butane gas lighter refills to 25ml because of the high proportion of VSA-related deaths in which they were implicated. The figures for 1997[7] show that VSA continues to take a heavy toll, with 73 deaths of which 41 (56%) had gas lighter refills implicated. The Government has been unable to secure industry-wide agreement to a 25ml maximum and cannot, because of European Union Single Market obligations, impose a maximum by law. We regret that, but welcome the Government's alternative – the introduction of an offence of the sale of these refills to those aged under 18, from 1 October 1999. It is important to try to prevent the refills getting into the hands of people who may be inclined to misuse them.

8.18   We believe that our central message on VSA in our earlier report that VSA was so dangerous it should not be practised, remains valid.

ADVICE ON ECSTASY

8.19   In the case of Ecstasy the Council has previously given advice about how the risks can be reduced (but not eliminated), which has become well-established and we will not repeat it here. It forms part of the message which the Health Education Authority and the Health Education Board for Scotland put out.

8.20   It seems now to be pretty well known that taking fluids and "chilling out" can help to reduce the risks of death through overheating and dehydration. But the risks are not eliminated and death may occur through other mechanisms also (see

Chapter 2). Its effects are likely to be potentiated by taking other drugs (including alcohol) at the same time. That danger should be emphasised.

PREVENTION OF IMMEDIATE DEATHS AND THE ROLE OF PARTICULAR AGENCIES

THE CRUCIAL ROLE OF DRUG SERVICES

8.21   Paragraphs 8.10–8.11 express our view on the need for services (and other bodies) to discourage injecting so as to reduce drug-related deaths. However, we believe that this is only part of a wider philosophy which all services should explicitly embrace. They should regard the prevention of deaths as one of their priority responsibilities, and this must be equally true in relation to prevention of immediate deaths and deaths due to chronic disease. It is implicit in much of the work which services do that their aims already include reducing drug-related deaths. But the principle needs to be more firmly established in the individual and institutional consciousness. Services for drug misusers are, of course, not a single uniform entity. Their make-up and functions vary and what follows will apply to any particular agency in varying degree. It will be for them, whether as individuals or organisations, to assess to what extent our suggestions and recommendations apply to their work. Services already do much good work for drug misusers but we believe that when it comes to reducing deaths among their clients or patients, there is scope for many of them to improve the way they work.

8.22   Consistent with the philosophy which we described in paragraph 8.21 we recommend that every service should develop and put in place an explicit policy to reduce drug-related deaths. Policies on reduction of immediate deaths should be developed within that context. It is the responsibility of these services to have such policies and DATs should assist and monitor their implementation.

THE NEED FOR POLICIES ON RISK ASSESSMENT

8.23   Supporting that approach, we see a need for a risk assessment to be undertaken for every drug misuser in contact with services. As part of the treatment plan, a person-specific intervention plan should be drawn up to minimise risk of immediate death (and death from chronic drug-related disease). We are sympathetic to time demands but must resist any plea that time pressures would make such work impossible. The assessment might take a standard structured form, modified according to the agency. It would represent good, professional, practice.

8.24   The assessment would embrace matters such as what drugs the client was using with opioids implying high risks; using drugs intravenously; sharing equipment; practising unprotected sex; using depressants at the same time as opioids; drinking alcohol at the same time; having a chaotic lifestyle; living in social isolation; a history of previous overdose; mental health problems; suicidal ideas expressed (even ambiguously); previously attempted suicide or oblivion sought through drug misuse; currently subject to negative life events (for example, appearing in court or separation from a partner); likely exposure to loss of tolerance, for example having been recently released from prison or institutional treatment; recent or current induction into methadone. The time and opportunity for assessing risk and implementing an intervention plan (see next paragraph) will be different for different services. Some will have only a fleeting opportunity while others will have considerable opportunity. The important thing is to take advantage of whatever situation presents itself. Where some form of assessment is a practical proposition, it should not be a one-off event but should form the start of a process of continuous assessment, with the intervention plan being adjusted as necessary in the light of it. Mental health services and drug services may wish to consult on approaches to risk assessment with their training and experience contributing mutually.

RISK ASSESSMENT SHOULD BE FOLLOWED BY IMPLEMENTATION OF AN ACTION PLAN

8.25   The information obtained would help the agency worker to draw up a specific intervention plan within the overall treatment plan, and which should be discussed with the client. The fact that the agency is taking prevention of death as a serious issue in itself will convey an important message to the client. That message must be presented as one of doing in partnership everything possible to reduce risk of death, but not the deceiving message that prevention of drug-related death can ever be guaranteed if injection is persisted with. We cannot say in this report what will be suitable for all clients but consideration should be given to how any injecting might be reduced or stopped; how concomitant antidepressant and alcohol consumption might be reduced; whether the prescription of benzodiazepines is appropriate; whether selective serotonin re-uptake inhibitors (SSRIs) would be better prescribed for depression than tricyclic anti-depressants (they usually will be); whether prescription of psychotropic drugs should be restricted in duration; whether methadone prescription is appropriate; whether psychiatric referral is necessary; or whether social services should be involved. A multidisciplinary response may often be required (see Annex 1 of the Guidelines on Clinical Management).

8.26   There are obvious training implications from these recommendations which will need to be followed through, and we recommend that they be met.

8.27   Risk assessment in every instance needs to be followed by a distinct course of action. We are concerned that over the prevention of drug-related deaths, some services have become complacent about reducing deaths among their patients or clients. We think that it is important that they and their staff remember that they are answerable for, so far as possible, preventing the deaths of their clients. They must avoid falling into the trap of believing that high rates of premature death are inevitable among drug users. They must accordingly avoid entering into a complicit relationship with clients which inhibits everyone concerned from trying to alter behaviour so as to reduce the risk of premature death.

8.28   On occasion overdose may occur on the premises of a drug agency. We believe therefore that staff should be trained in resuscitation techniques and nalaxone kept on site.

THE RESPONSIBILITY TO PREVENT DIVERSION OF PRESCRIBED DRUGS

8.29   In the preceding paragraphs we have pointed to those things which we believe drug services should be doing to reduce deaths from drug misuse. Drug services also need to recognise that they have public health responsibilities which go beyond their immediate client or patient group. For example, they need to consider whether drugs which they prescribe are likely to be diverted to the illicit market and to take steps to avoid it occurring. Drug misusers have responsibilities to others too, and should be encouraged to avoid putting others at risk of premature death by their actions. For example, injectors should be encouraged not to initiate others into injecting, and those on prescribed controlled drugs should be reminded of the need to exercise care when carrying them home and to store them safely so they cannot be ingested by children.

DRUGS SERVICES, MENTAL HEALTH AND SUICIDE PREVENTION

8.30   In Chapter 3, poor mental health, particularly depression, was identified as a frequent occurrence among drug users. The mental health of drug users is an important factor which has implications for the role of services.

8.31   There is one element of risk among drug misusers that we would particularly draw attention to, and that is suicide[8]. It is within the drug misuse perspective a rather neglected subject.

8.32   There is no doubt that depressive illness (major psychological depression) and the availability of drugs, especially mixtures of drugs, greatly enhance the likelihood of suicide. But at the moment both drugs services and general mental health services regard the two conditions, drug misuse and depression, as separate issues. We believe that broad improvement in the quality and connectedness of treatment services would be likely to reduce suicides. Accordingly we recommend that both drug and general mental health services should strengthen their abilities to deal with misusers who have mental health problems.

8.33   In practical terms this means both types of service needing to improve their assessment and management of suicide risk among drugs users. That, in turn, will require training and the development of validated assessment protocols. These are matters which the National Institute of Clinical Excellence might encourage. And we believe that drug and general mental health services should establish liaison links with one another. There may be a role for DATs, and DAATs in Wales, in helping to forge them. Drugs users in our view deserve full access to help with mental health and any barriers relating to stigma should be overcome.

8.34   We would refer back to paragraph 3.37 and 8.25 and emphasise the need to consider whether for drug users it would generally be safer to prescribe for depression SSRIs, rather than tricyclic anti-depressants.

PREVENTION OF DRUG-RELATED DEATHS AND THE ROLE OF PRIMARY CARE

8.35   The role of general practitioners, pharmacists and the increasing number of generalist and specialist nursing colleagues in the primary health care team, provide an important opportunity for preventing and reducing deaths from taking drugs. What we say in this section is equally applicable to prevention of suicide and virus transmission.

8.36   Knowledge of domestic or family circumstances should give the primary care worker opportunities for assessment of high risk of deaths from drug misuse. This might be indicated by excessive chaotic drug use, or repeated presentation with lack of resolution of the problem, giving rise to the need for reassessment. There may be several ways forward including consideration of:

- An inappropriate level of prescribing, including the possibility that the dose of the prescribed drug is too low;

- The use of additional street drugs such as stimulants causing behavioural difficulties and problems;

- The presence of an additional diagnosis such as depression or psychosis requiring further specialist referral.

8.37   General practitioners, especially those prescribing for opioid dependent patients, should have close working relationships with community pharmacies, leading to sensitivity and flexibility in individual cases. There should on occasion be some relaxation of the stringent regulations for dispensing under the Misuse of Drugs Act 1971, as recommended by the Royal Pharmaceutical Society[9]. But prescribing doctors and community pharmacists have an obligation to observe local and national guidelines and to regularly update their knowledge and take advantage of local training. Multidisciplinary training would be particularly advantageous.

8.38   Specific interventions available to primary care include:

- testing for blood-borne viruses

- providing needles, syringes and other paraphernalia

- being aware of dangerous injecting when it is present

- assisting injectors to get away from the needle habit

- encouraging involvement in self help groups

- prescribing and administering hepatitis B vaccine

- proper assessment of risk of suicide

- response to overdoses and other emergencies

- warning patients about the dangers of driving under the influence of prescribed and illegal drugs and possibly taking action to notify DVLA when these warnings are not noted

ACCIDENT AND EMERGENCY DEPARTMENTS

8.39   Among the services which come into contact with drug misusers, Accident and Emergency (A&E) departments play an important role. Depending on their location, they will periodically treat people who have overdosed on opioids, whether those overdoses are deliberate or not. A & E departments are busy places with a high turnover of staff. However, the fact that they see overdosers who have not died and who are subsequently discharged, is an opportunity which we think must be exploited more vigorously. Many such attenders are repeat attenders. While A and E departments are geared to get patients over the immediate crisis, we think that hospitals should have arrangements in place to ensure that the treatment or advice needs of such patients are picked up after discharge. The principal care worker, often the GP, should be informed of the incident. At a minimum, cards should be handed out which give simple advice on what help is available with appropriate local contact information, and advice to help shift the person away from injecting and in other ways decrease the likelihood of death. DATs should play a part in establishing the necessary arrangements.

EMERGENCY SERVICES, THEIR RESPONSE TO OVERDOSES, AND THE RESPONSE OF PEOPLE WHO WITNESS THE OVERDOSE

8.40   We have so far covered those aspects of drug misuse which are susceptible to some form of initiative which will help to reduce the possibility of overdose occurring. We now turn to the situation where overdose has occurred and what can be done to prevent death being the consequence.

8.41 A & E departments treat an enormous range of ailments and opioid overdosers will represent a small but varying proportion depending on the locality. We think it would be inappropriate for us to attempt to say what staff training or treatment protocols are appropriate for treating this kind of emergency in this setting but we do believe that hospitals should satisfy themselves that the arrangements are satisfactory. The possible role of the Resuscitation Council in regard to this issue should be explored.

8.42 When a drug user overdoses or reacts badly to a drug, it is not unusual for there to be someone else present. This is often another drug user. Their response can be important in determining whether an overdose leads to death. Most people who die from an overdose, do so before reaching hospital. Identifying whether someone has overdosed may itself be difficult or the other people present may, through their own drug misuse, have impaired judgement or perception. Even when overdose is identified, witnesses may be reluctant to call an ambulance for fear that the police will also become involved, and prosecution under some heading ensue. Our view is that a call to a person who has overdosed should be regarded by the ambulance and police services as a *medical emergency* in the first instance, rather than as a call to the scene of a crime. It follows that we do not believe that ambulance services should, as a matter of course, inform the police when they are called to a drug overdose. We understand that currently some services do and some do not. There will be cause for the ambulance service to do so upon arrival at the scene if someone is dead. When there is evidence that children or other vulnerable persons are being subject to harm, or if the ambulance crew fear they may be attacked, are other examples where they may decide to involve the police. But we think that is as far as ambulance service policy should go. We suspect that fear of arrest sometimes deters appropriate help-seeking by those present and involved in drug use with the person who has overdosed. We recommend that, through DATs and their member agencies, agreed local policy is developed along the lines we suggest, and with this policy disseminated to drug users through local drug service and media mechanisms. Each individual situation is different and emergency services must retain the capacity to respond flexibly. We think it is probably unrealistic to expect police forces to give a blanket guarantee that witnesses to an overdose will not be prosecuted if officers attend. On the other hand, we think that should be the general presumption.

8.43 Part of the advice to drug users should be that it is safer to inject in the company of others rather than alone, with care that this message is not taken as implying that 'safer' means 'safe'. And there will be no advantage unless witnesses know what best to do in the event of an overdose, and are willing to do it. Research undertaken for us by Professor John Strang and Dr David Best at the Maudsley Hospital, London has provided some indicative data on this point. Expressed on the basis of response percent for number of overdoses witnessed 50% of the 155 subjects interviewed had responded by slapping the victim; 41% by walking them round the room; 36% by putting the victim into the recovery position; 35% by calling an ambulance; 33% by giving the kiss of life; and only 25% by calling an ambulance and waiting for it to arrive. We believe that heroin and other opioid users, who are most likely to be witnesses to their friends' overdoses, should be given guidance on what to do in those circumstances. We suggest that guidance should comprise calling an ambulance without delay, preferably remaining with the casualty until help arrives, and (whether they stay until help has arrived or not), providing basic first aid in terms of putting the person in the recovery position and ensuring nothing is blocking their mouth or throat. This guidance is something else which we would expect services in contact with misusers to accomplish.

8.44   There will, of course, be a stage in overdose between attendance of the ambulance (or paramedic), and admission to an Accident and Emergency department. As we said above in relation to A & E departments, we do not think it is appropriate for us to say what training should be given and what protocols should apply. But we believe that ambulance and paramedic services should satisfy themselves that the arrangements for preventing deaths from overdose are robust.

8.45   In one particular respect we do, however, believe that the response of ambulance services could be improved. As we understand it all ambulances do not routinely carry the drug naloxone, nor are members of staff other than paramedics, trained to administer, naloxone. We understand that there is variation in these regards across the country. It is a specific and effective but short-acting antidote to opioid overdose. We believe that it should be included among these services' available treatment responses in all localities. Clearly the staff concerned would continue to give priority attention to secure airways and other routine matters and the effort to locate a vein for injection of naloxone should not be allowed to stand in the way of good routine practice.

8.46   A question then arises as to whether naloxone should be made more generally available, for example, to those who are likely to witness opioid overdoses[10]. This would involve a supply of the drug being kept at home, and advice being given to friends and partners of the drug users on its emergency use. As well as close associates of the user, naloxone might also be made available to prison healthcare staff. And it should be kept at police stations which have custody suites for emergency use by medical staff and other trained personnel. We appreciate that this will require some relaxation of the current Medicines Act 1968.

8.47   Such a course might possibly give rise to a perception that there was connivance in, or encouragement of, drug taking. If it was accepted that this wider availability of naloxone was desirable there would be a need to ensure, through training, that the drug was administered correctly and in the right circumstances; that it was seen only as part of a larger resuscitative response; that fresh supplies were regularly introduced; and that proper arrangements were in place for its prescription, including to whom it might be administered.

8.48   Our view is that, as a matter of principle, naloxone should be made more widely available (that is beyond hospital, paramedic and ambulance settings), but that in doing so careful consideration should be given to issues which we have raised in the previous paragraph.

8.49   As drugs other than naloxone are developed as antidotes to opioid overdose, they may prove more suitable.

PENAL AND ENFORCEMENT SERVICES

POLICE ARRESTEES

8.50   On one recent estimate a high proportion (about 60% on average) of people who are arrested by the police test positive for drugs[11]. Of those about 20% tested positive for opiates, although there were wide regional variations. However, if the police should suspect someone of being a drug taker in the normal course of their work whether a police surgeon (or forensic medical examiner) will be called, is largely at the discretion of the custody officer and it is not routine. However, we see some scope for intervention by a police surgeon which might help reduce deaths. We appreciate that police surgeons are busy, and their main purpose is to establish if the arrestee is fit enough to be detained and interviewed. Nonetheless, the contact which they have with the arrestee, who may well not be in contact with treatment services but would consider treatment, is an opportunity which should not be missed. The police surgeon should suggest to the arrestee that a referral to services may be appropriate, and that they speak to the Custody Officer about such a referral. The Council made a similar point in its report on Police, Drug Misusers and the Community[12]. Improvements seem most likely to be possible if the training for police surgeons incorporates mention of the role which they can play in reducing drug-related deaths. This is an issue which might usefully be addressed by the Home Office Working Group on Police Surgeons which is expected to issue its report in the near future. We commend the development of Drug Arrest Referral Schemes, a partnership initiative which encourages drug misusers in contact with the police service, voluntarily to participate in confidential programmes of advice, information and treatment. These schemes are now extending to referral from all areas of the criminal justice system. There may be local leaflets about these schemes available for any person in need.

8.51   There are examples of arrestees having died in police custody following cocaine induced delirium, and we recommend that police forces are given guidance on how to identify and deal with these cases.

PRISONS AND AFTERCARE

8.52   In its 1996 report "Drug Misusers and the Prison System – An Integrated Approach"[13] the Council made recommendations on the transition of prisoners back into the community (paragraphs 6.38–6.43). They were that:

- preparations for release should start at the beginning of the period of custody

- better links should be made between the field and prison and probation staff over detailed release arrangements, including links into drug-related services, and

- health and local authorities should agree responsibilities together within the context of the local drug strategy, and that where this proves difficult Drug Action Teams should act to ensure that all relevant agencies agree adequate funding of services to prisons

The recommendations remain relevant but regrettably do not appear to have been acted on at the time. However, recently, at the beginning of October 1999, the Prison Service in England and Wales introduced at all establishments for all drug users who require this type of help, Counselling, Assessment, Referral and Advice and Treatment (the CARAT scheme). The services are provided by outside contractors to a detailed specification. The expectations appear to be comprehensive and if properly implemented could considerably help to reduce deaths among people who are or have been imprisoned. We hope that the near future will see this scheme properly and comprehensively implemented.

8.53   In one respect we would go further than the previous report. Our strong impression, still, is that prison services, commissioning bodies and drug services have not served prisoners and released prisoners well. Too often we have seen complex arrangements for funding, treatment and care create obstacles for people and organisations. Some drug services have sought to work with prisons but found it difficult to engage with them. Proper links must be made to ensure that prisoners on release are not put in a vulnerable position. The provision of early care on release is an opportunity to minimise the risk of overdose and relapse, and one which should not be missed. We see a considerable role for DATs, and DAATs in Wales, in ensuring that effective joint commissioning and sound operational links are made.

8.54   There is a small number of opioid-related deaths in prison in England and Wales (two or less in each of the last three years). A report on a series of suicides in Cortonvale, Scotland's only prison for women, concluded that drug withdrawals played an important part in most of them[14]. There has been some suggestion that withdrawal symptoms may increase the risk of suicide. In treating drug misusers in prisons this possibility should be borne in mind.

8.55   The fact that loss of tolerance is a contributory factor to the risk of death after release, raises questions about the appropriateness of automatic detoxification of prisoners. In some circumstances, for example, where a short-term prisoner is under methadone treatment on admission, it may be sensible to continue to prescribe it to him or her. There could be advantages for the patient in terms of stability, quite apart from helping to reduce the risk of overdose on release. Among the 64 fatal drug misuse related overdoses in Greater Glasgow recorded by Strathclyde Police in the first nine months of 1999, 24% occurred within two weeks of release from prison[15].

PREVENTING DEATHS FROM TRAFFIC ACCIDENTS AND VIOLENCE

ROAD TRAFFIC ACCIDENTS

8.56   The very fact of taking drugs causes people to lose their sense of judgement. It follows that they open themselves up to a higher risk of fatal accident to themselves and maybe other people, depending on where they are and what they do. Given the prevalence of motor vehicle driving it is here that there is greatest concern. Government studies suggest that among accidents involving fatalities, drugs have been found in 15–20% of riders and drivers[16]. That is not to say that the presence of the drug has necessarily contributed to the accident, but the figures give cause for concern. It is already an offence to drive while unfit through drugs, whether prescribed or not, and the Government should continue to bring home the message that taking drugs and driving is reckless. Treatment agencies should be more active in bringing the risks of drugged-driving to the attention of their clients. We welcome the attempts that are being made to develop for the police methods of identifying drivers who are unfit through drugs.

HOMICIDES

8.57   Drugs are implicated in some homicides, in terms of dealers acting violently and killing rivals or innocent bystanders. It is possible that intoxication with stimulant drugs or with hallucinogens may, in rare instances, be a factor contributing to disinhibited and dangerous behaviour. Paradoxical excitement can occur with benzodiazepines. While not dismissing such possibilities, we note that hard evidence on causality as opposed to association underlying the relationship between drug misuse and violence, is slight. If a client has a known history of violence and is taking certain drugs, the risks should however at least be considered by any agency which is treating that individual, and appropriate steps taken where possible. The drug which carries most danger of violence is of course alcohol.

8.58   The Scottish Prison Service has also had a policy on the management of drug misusers in prison since 1994 which emphasises the importance of warning prisons of the dangers of overdose due to loss of tolerance following resumption of drug taking on release. Since 1998, all prisons in Scotland have been supplied with credit card-sized wallets with information about how to avoid overdose. These are to be given to known drug misusers shortly before release. The Scottish Prison Service Policy has also sanctioned the continuation of methadone for prisoners on short sentences or on remand when supported by the prisoner's general practitioner. In practice however, this has rarely happened. New clinical guidelines on the management of drug misuse in prison issued in 1999 should improve the situation.

CONCLUSIONS

8.59   We believe that building on the current good work of numerous agencies and of GPs, there is a wide spectrum of measures which can be put in place to reduce the incidence of immediate drug-related deaths. Each measure taken by itself, whether small or large, can make a useful contribution. But if these measures are brought to bear on the problem in concert, we would expect before long to see a fall in these kinds of death. We hesitate to offer any exact quantification of what would be achieved but believe that an intensive, broad and sustained initiative of the kind we propose, would save a very considerable number of lives.

9 REDUCING DEATHS FROM CHRONIC ILLNESSES

Prevention of virus infections must be a key component in the prevention of drug-related deaths, and a response to hepatitis C and B is now needed of a scope equal to the responses to HIV.

TAKING THE PROBLEM SERIOUSLY

9.1   In the public mind the phrase "deaths from drug misuse" will still most probably suggest fatalities resulting from overdose, or from other acute consequences of the individual's drug taking. There is likely also to be some consciousness of the relevance of HIV. But awareness of the threat posed by chronic illnesses resulting from hepatitis infections is still far too poorly developed. With HIV and hepatitis B and hepatitis C, it is factors such as the protracted latency, the uncertainty and variation in the disease progression, and the fact that a single careless injection can lead to someone's death as much as 30 or 40 years later, that may all conspire to keep the threats out of sharp focus and encourage their neglect. Some other infections also need to be considered but at the moment it is HIV and the hepatitis viruses which are the main causes.

9.2   As corrective to that neglect, we see it as appropriate at the outset of this chapter to state fairly and squarely our belief that virus infections among drug misusers should now be seen as cause for intense public health concern, and a determined new initiative of appropriate scope. As year after year, cohort after cohort of drug users are infected with one or other or several of these viruses (and risk of infection does not stop with enrolment at a DDU), so the burden piles up for the future. An infected drug user may stop their drug use, but their virus infection will stay with them as legacy of their drug-using days. Not only are these virus infections likely to contribute with increasing significance to the overall mortality rates among drug users, but the treatment of the diseases to which the viruses give rise, is likely along the way to result in immense costs to the National Health Service. And as well as drug users themselves being at risk, there are risks of sexual transmission to partners, and if there is maternal infection there is risk of virus transmission to children.

THE EXTENT OF THE PROBLEM

9.3   We hesitate to offer any quantitative projections on the probable level of virus-related deaths which will be occurring among drug-users (or former drug-users) at any future time-point. Too many of the variables are undetermined and the situation may in the long term get worse or better. That no kind of projection can be given in the face of this threatening public health problem is, however, in itself worrying. The country is encountering an immensely threatening public health problem without the data with which to monitor population trends and the effectiveness of policies.

THE VIRUSES

9.4   As background for understanding some of the underlying-medical issues relating to the virus infections which can result from drug injecting[1], Table 9.1 offers a summary tabulation. Different viruses are different, but they can to an extent be viewed within a common framework.

Table 9.1 Hepatitis C infection among a community wide sample of injectors in Greater Glasgow by year when first injected

Year began injecting	Number tested	Number positive	% Positive
1996	55	27	49
1997	59	20	34
1998	72	16	22
1999	31	3	10

9.5   It is important to note the difference between the detection of markers of infection on the one hand, and viral carriage rates on the other. The former refers to evidence of current infection with a virus or evidence of previous exposure. The detection of antibody to hepatitis C (anti-HCV) or antibody to the core antigen of hepatitis B (anti-HBc), give this information. The viral carriage refers to the detection of evidence that virus or viral components are being produced in the patient at the time of testing. The detection of hepatitis B surface antigen (HBsAg) defines hepatitis B carriage, and hepatitis C RNA (HCV-RNA) is detected in hepatitis C carriers.

9.6   It is a salient difference between hepatitis B and C that only 5% of adults infected with hepatitis B develop long term viral carriage, whereas as many as 80% of those exposed to hepatitis C may carry the virus long term[2].

9.7   In the last two years two further blood transmitted hepatitis viruses have been described. Both hepatitis G virus[3] and the transfusion transmitted virus (TTV)[4], are found more frequently in drug users than in members of the general population. The impact of these viruses on the health of carriers is as yet unclear but is unlikely to be as significant as hepatitis B or C.

HIV

9.8   Data currently available on deaths from virus-related causes due to earlier drug injecting, are for HIV, and come from the Communicable Disease Surveillance Centre and the Scottish Centre for Environmental Health[5]. In 1997 (the latest year for which data are available), 69 out of the 638 HIV-related deaths were recorded as having had injecting drug use as an antecedent. By the end of 1998, there had been 279 reported deaths of injecting drug users with AIDS in Scotland, representing almost 40% of all the AIDS deaths in Scotland[6].

PREVENTION OF HIV INFECTION

9.9   We do not intend to revisit the subject of HIV/AIDS in detail, because the Council has already produced three reports on this subject[7,8,9]. However, there is need for some up-dating notes.

9.10   Crucially, we believe that this country has over recent years achieved an important measure of success in curtailing the rates of HIV occurring among injecting drug users[10-11]. Among injectors drug users having a named HIV test, the positivity rate in Lothian has fallen from 9% in 1989 to 0.6% in 1997. In Greater Glasgow the positivity rate has remained at between 0.5% and 1.5% during the same period[12]. Cause and effect cannot be strictly proved in the absence of controlled trials, but it seems likely that the total mix of harm minimisation strategies which were put in place in the late 1980s and the scale of their availability, have to an extent succeeded in stemming the HIV epidemic among injecting drug users. This history is of such potential importance to understanding the relevant public health issues that we urge further investment in its close analysis.

9.11   Policies to reduce the spread of HIV among injecting drug users are bound also to have some impact on diseases which are transmitted in a similar way. Conversely, as we consider in the next section how deaths from hepatitis C can be reduced, our recommendations may have some additional impact on HIV related deaths.

9.12   An important development since Council last reported on AIDS is the availability of more effective drug treatments for HIV/AIDS. The newly available regimens for HIV management including the recently developed protease inhibitors, have been shown to improve the short term survival of AIDS sufferers. However, the development of strains of the virus resistant to treatment is increasingly common and their long term impact remains to be evaluated. (Table 9.2)

Table 9.2

Virus	Effect	Transmission route	Infectivity	Chronicity	Recommendations for Inactivation	Estimated risk of premature death	Treatment	Vaccine	Prevention
HIV	Damages immune system causing AIDS	Blood to blood contact, sexual intercourse, mother to child	Low Infectivity by needle contact	Most infections long term	Dilute bleach will inactivate	90–95% but modified by recent treatment advances	Numerous new agents under trial	None	Safe sex Discourage injection Clean Works
Hepatitis B	Liver inflammation Leading to Cirrhosis and	Blood to blood contact, sexual intercourse, mother to child	High risk by needle contact with infectious carrier	5% adults develop long term infection		If chronic carrier 20% may develop cirrhosis and/or liver cancer	Interferon and newer agents effective in 30-40% of chronic carriers	Highly effective and widely available	Vaccination Safe sex Discourage injection Clean works
Hepatitis C	Liver cancer	Blood to blood contact. Other routes rare	Moderate to high risk by needle contact	70–80% develop long term infection	Undiluted bleach for 1 minute	20% in chronic carrier	Interferon + ribavirin effective in 40-50%	None	Discourage injection Clean works

HEPATITIS C

9.13   Among current injecting drug users in England and Wales 57% are HCV positive[13–14], with 68% being found positive in Scotland[15]. In Great Britain estimates for the number of former and present injectors who are infected with HCV range between 152,000 and 228,000 according to the assumptions which are made, and around either of those figures there are wide margins of uncertainty[16]. Even read with all due caution, these projections of HCV prevalence amply justify anxiety about the size of the public problem which is on the horizon.

9.14   Alarming evidence of hepatitis C infection among new heroin injectors comes from a recent survey of drug injectors in Glasgow[17]. During the first half of 1999, a total of 217 individuals who reported starting to inject since the beginning of 1996 were recruited from a wide range of community locations, needle exchanges and drug services. Each respondent answered a questionnaire and provided a saliva sample for hepatitis C testing. Of the 217, 66 (30%) tested positive. Table 9.2 shows that the infection rate ranged from 49% among those starting to inject in 1996 to 10% among those starting in 1999. These data provide evidence of hepatitis C infection occurring soon after injecting begins. Equally disturbing are the large numbers of people recruited to the study who clearly only started injecting within the past 18 months. This points to a new wave of heroin injecting with all the attendant risks of death and other serious health problems. We also have available a pre-publication copy of a report from Dr Vivian Hope and his colleagues[18], who looked at the HCV status of drug injectors in England and Wales. These authors tested 2203 drug injectors recruited from agencies and 758 not in contact with agencies over the previous 4 weeks. Sharing of injecting equipment during the previous month was reported by 44% and 42% of the two groups respectively. Positive virus status was significantly related to duration of injecting. HCV positivity increased from 7.4% among those injecting for less than 3 years to 62% in those injecting for 15 years or more. For HBV the corresponding rates were 5.2% and 52%. Overall rates for HIV were less than 1%. The estimated annual incidence of HCV for those who started to inject in the last two years was less than 5%.

9.15   Recent data from the United States[19] gives grave cause for concern with regard to the prevalence of hepatitis C. It has been estimated that 1.8% of the population have hepatitis C infection, and this infection is most commonly associated with use of drugs.

9.16   Hepatitis C is highly infectious by blood to blood contact. While our principal interest is to prevent transmission through drug-associated means, it is worth noting that, although it would be unusual, the disease is transmissible through blood to blood contact of open cuts, tattooing, body piercing and bites. Sexual transmission is not common. The prospect of developing a vaccine to prevent infection appears in the foreseeable future to be remote. (Table 9.2)

9.17   The highly infectious nature of the virus goes some way to explaining the high prevalence of the disease among injecting drug users. Any occasion of drug misuse involving injecting where any part of the process is shared, gives rise to a very real risk of the disease being transmitted if one of the participants is already infected. Given the prevalence of infection among existing injecting drug users and that the first occasion of injection is likely to be a shared experience, that fact is very worrying: it calls into question whether enough is being done to prevent infection at this initial stage. In Chapter 8 we have already said that it is essential that non-injectors are encouraged never to inject, and that message is of course highly relevant to the concerns of this chapter. The nature of HCV infectivity supports the conclusion that there is a need to discourage injecting at every opportunity. It is no good waiting until the first referral to a DDU for the first health message to be given.

9.18   Among prospective injectors and those who do inject efforts need to be made to dissuade them from doing so and, failing that, the importance of ensuring absolute cleanliness during each injection needs to be emphasised. The infectivity of hepatitis C is such that sharing any items involved in the process – needles, syringes, water, filters, or spoons or other vessels – opens the risk of infection.

9.19   Previously used equipment needs to be effectively decontaminated. The hepatitis C virus is more robust than the HIV virus. The minimum decontamination procedure involves soaking the equipment (needles, syringes, plungers, spoons or other hardware) in neat household bleach for at least one minute, followed by a good rinsing in clean water. Fresh bleach should be used on each occasion. Those following this procedure should take care to keep the bleach well out of the reach of children.

9.20   Although transmission of hepatitis C between sexual partners is uncommon, it is sensible to encourage use of condoms to minimise any risk of transmission from an HCV carrier. As HCV can be detected in the saliva of chronic carriers it is also recommended that carriers do not share toothbrushes. This may be particularly true for those with poor oral hygiene as they would be more likely to experience bleeding in the mouth due to gum infections.

9.21   Among people who develop antibodies following exposure to the hepatitis C virus around 70–80% remain infectious and at risk of long-term sequelae of their infection. It is estimated that as many as 20% of these will eventually develop cirrhosis or cancer of the liver over the following decades[20].

9.22   Currently available treatment for hepatitis C with a combination of interferon and ribavirin, may lead to long term loss of virus from the blood in 40–50% of those treated[21]. Loss of virus is associated with improvement in the appearance of the liver under the microscope, and arrest in the progression of the disease. The other principal intervention which can reduce the rate of progression of the disease is cutting back on alcohol intake or, preferably, abstaining from alcohol. The success of these interventions is greater the earlier the infection is diagnosed. The Council in Chapter 8 of its third report on AIDS and drug misuse[9] recommended:

- the expansion of opportunities for voluntary HIV testing which is accessible and appropriate to clients' needs, accompanied by counselling and support from adequately trained staff;

- a more proactive approach to testing in areas of known or suspected high prevalence, targeting the provision of testing at people who engage in high risk behaviours;

- more widespread use of anonymised HIV prevalence surveys.

We believe those recommendations apply equally to hepatitis B and C.

9.23   Those found to be infected with hepatitis C should be referred to a hepatologist for advice about further management and treatment.

HEPATITIS B

9.24   As with hepatitis C, infection with hepatitis B can give rise to chronic disease and cause death long after the initial infection, but the course is generally less malign. About 5% of hepatitis B infected individuals will become long term carriers of the virus, and of these 15–20% will develop chronic hepatitis with risks of cirrhosis or liver cancer[22]. (Table 9.2)

9.25   In that hepatitis B is rather easily transmitted sexually as well as by injecting, the partners of injecting drug users as well as users themselves may need to be tested.

9.26   Unlike with hepatitis C, a vaccine to protect against hepatitis B is available. A course of treatment (3 injections with the vaccine) costs about £40.00, a trivial demand on health service resources compared with the potential costs of treating the disease if contacted. We fully support the following advice offered in the recent Department of Health Guidelines on Clinical Management of Drug Misuse and Drug Dependence:

> "Immunisation for hepatitis B is recommended for injecting drug misusers not already infected or immune, and for close household contacts, particularly the sexual partners of any injecting drug misusers already infected. It is good practice to be pro-active in offering immunisation to all these groups."[23]

9.27   However, as exposure to hepatitis B is likely to occur early in an injecting career and, before contact is made with drug services, the only certain way of preventing this infection from being transmitted would be to include vaccination as part of the universal childhood vaccination programme. This is the approach recommended by the World Health Organisation[24] and adopted in the majority of European Countries and in North America.

9.28   In the past, many intravenous drug users who were carriers of hepatitis B became infected with an associated virus called hepatitis D or Delta virus. Transmission is by blood to blood contact. As this virus can only infect hepatitis B carriers it can be prevented by hepatitis B vaccination. It may lead to an acceleration of the liver disease caused by hepatitis B which may be fatal.

9.29   Specialist advice on the treatment of hepatitis B infected drug users should be sought from a hepatologist. Interferon may again have something to offer in selected instances, and liver transplant may eventually be indicated if cirrhosis has developed.

OTHER TYPES OF INFECTION WHICH MAY BE TRANSMITTED BY OR ASSOCIATED WITH DRUG MISUSE

9.30   In Chapter 2 we noted that drug injectors are exposed to the risk of septicaemia and consequent infection of the heart valves, and this may result in death some or many years later. The relevance for helping agencies is the implicit need for alertness and for good liaison with physical medicine.

DRUG MISUSE AND VIRUS INFECTIONS: CROSS-CUTTING ELEMENTS IN STRENGTHENING THE HELPING AGENCY RESPONSES

9.31   Across the spectrum of HIV, hepatitis B and hepatitis C, helping agencies, whether statutory or voluntary, have a highly important role in prevention of drug-related deaths due to chronic disease, primarily by their contribution to prevention of these virus infections, and secondly by ensuring early and appropriate referral to specialist treatment. These are however problems for which primary prevention is likely to be very much better than cure.

9.32   Besides the measures outlined in Chapter 8, some of the ways in which we believe that the agencies' contributions to work on prevention of deaths from chronic drug-related deaths should now be strengthened, include the following. Again, in making these recommendations we are aware that good work is already being done.

• Enhanced staff training is often likely to be needed to meet the needs implicit in the demands identified here. Such training should be nationally available, and its quality, comprehensiveness and availability should be audited.

• Agencies should ensure that screening for virus infections is routinely and appropriately used, with pre- and post-test counselling on the implications of results. It cannot be assumed that virus positivity will automatically lead to change in equipment-sharing or sexual practices, but effort must be made to help infected users away from behaviours which put other people at risk.

• Information should be given to drug injectors on optimum measures for sterilising injecting equipment with these measures adequate for hepatitis C. The message should at the same time be repeated that no injecting can ever be guaranteed to be safe.

• Health authorities should take all reasonable steps to ensure that sufficient supplies of clean injecting equipment are readily accessible to all drug injectors. All clients at needle exchanges should be encouraged to hand in all their used injecting equipment for safe disposal.

• Although not guaranteed free of germs, fresh tap or bottled water is not in itself a source of hepatitis C or other bloodborne viruses. If supplies of sterile water are made available they should always be in the form of individual doses in plastic ampoules to avoid possible cross-contamination.

• Agencies which provide treatment or counselling for drug users should have liaison with, and input from, professionals with specialist knowledge of the virus diseases and there should be ready pathways for referral.

9.33   But whatever the detail of the actions required, we see it as necessary to work toward an overall change in awareness so as to make prevention of chronic virus-related illnesses and associated deaths (and not just HIV) an ongoing, priority part of such agencies' work. That will mean training and staff awareness, protocols to ensure good practice, stated agency policies, audit, and a determination to ensure that prevention messages are delivered skilfully and persuasively and held in place. DATs have a responsibility to ensure that this happens.

PRISONS AND THE PREVENTION OF VIRUS INFECTIONS

9.34   The Council in previous reports[9,25] has pointed to the significance of imprisonment as an opportunity for interventions with drug misusers. We have also referred in Chapter 8 to the need for transition back into the community to be better managed, in order to reduce deaths from the immediate effects of taking drugs. Added cogency attaches to those recommendations in the light of the matters we have discussed in the present chapter. Inertia of any kind would be expensive and damaging.

9.35   The Council in its report, Drug Misusers and the Prison System[25] (paragraph 9.20), recommended that renewed efforts were made through continually updated education programmes, to inform staff and prisoners about the risk of transmission of all blood-borne viruses. That recommendation remains as germane now as it was then.

9.36   We understand that the Prison Service in England and Wales, and the Scottish Prison Service, have undertaken pilot studies in a number of prisons on the effectiveness of distributing disinfecting tablets in order to reduce transmission of infection. We commend efforts which lead to decontaminants being made widely available but this must be coupled with instructions on their use, as well as advice against injecting.

9.37   The Council concluded in its 1996 report[25], that needle exchange in prisons was not a practical proposition. Greater availability could increase intimidation of staff and prisoners; it was difficult to see how possession of a syringe could be condoned when both possession of injecting equipment and testing positive for drugs were disciplinary offences. There were legal as well as practical problems in setting exchanges up in an era of mandatory drug testing. We would not at present go back from that conclusion but if studies currently underway demonstrate a high rate of hepatitis C transmission in prison, a fresh initiative may be needed in this area.

9.38   The importance of offering hepatitis B vaccination to all prison entrants is emphasised. Although this is a current recommendation to prison medical officers, we understand that it is not always adhered to.

CONCLUSION

9.39   At worst, there is symmetry between the injector's belief that a virus infection "can't happen to me" and their dealing with the injecting habit postponed until too late, and public belief that preventing the societal problem set by drug-related-virus transmission can be postponed. We suggest that much which is beneficial can be learnt from the determined response to the HIV and drugs connection which has been mounted over the last ten years. But further action across the whole range of injection-related virus diseases is now urgently required, and should not be postponed.

10 PRIORITIES FOR A POLICY FRAMEWORK

This final chapter makes suggestions as to how action at many different front lines can be given coherence and common purpose with an overall policy framework. That framework will support the national initiative on prevention of drug-related deaths for which this report calls.

THE NEED FOR A POLICY FRAMEWORK

10.1 This report has made many separate recommendations directed at people and agencies who bear a wide range of different responsibilities in this field, and who between them have enormous opportunity to reduce the occurrence of drug-related deaths. Those recommendations are set out explicitly in the "Summary and Recommendations" section which precedes the main text.

10.2 In this final chapter we suggest how the diverse needed actions at so many different front lines, can be given cohesion and common purpose within an overall policy framework for an initiative on the prevention of drug-related deaths. We are not here going to repeat all the detail which has gone before, but will try to make the shape of what is needed stand out clearly, and will indicate some priorities. The Government's overall drugs strategy provides the larger context. Continued efforts directed at primary prevention and access to high-quality care will, for instance, give vital support to the specifics of the initiative which we are now proposing.

10.3 We identify the major elements within an effective, integrated policy as comprising at least the following:–

- A specification of data needs, and an improvement in the data system and its operational use at national and local level.

- A better informed public awareness of the nature and seriousness of the problem set by drug-related deaths.

- That awareness to embrace both acute drug-related deaths and those resulting from chronic illness.

- A heightened level of knowledge and commitment, and a shift in attitude toward drug-related deaths, across all relevant agencies.

- Improvement in relevant practices across agencies and audit of performance.

- Agency practices and policies to be aimed strongly and persistently at reducing injecting drug use.

- An end to lax or irresponsible prescribing and a radical curtailment of methadone-related deaths.

- A strengthened response to drug misuse by the prison service.

- Better liaison between agencies.

- The need to target social deprivation.

- Enhanced investment in professional training.

- Attempts actively to involve drug users themselves in responsibility for reducing drug-related deaths.

- A more determined attempt to reach drug users who are outside agency contact.

- Response to the needs of families.

- A crucial role for DATs and DAATs and their member agencies.

- Better investment in research which can help prevent drug-related deaths.

10.4   In the paragraphs below we give in sequence brief notes on each of these elements which will contribute to the building of a strong and integrated policy response.

IMPROVEMENT IN THE DATA SYSTEM AND IN ITS OPERATIONAL USE AT NATIONAL AND LOCAL LEVEL

10.5   The policies we envisage must be supported by a clearer definition of data needs, and by reliable data which can help monitor policy effectiveness and focus their application. We see a strengthening in the data base as vital to the policy frame both in terms of national action, and action within communities, where ways of using the data effectively will need increasingly to be explored.

A BETTER INFORMED PUBLIC AWARENESS OF THE PROBLEM SET BY DRUG-RELATED DEATHS.

10.6   We believe that a heightened public understanding of the importance and nature of the problems being addressed will be very generally helpful in supporting the needed initiatives and the work of those who will bear responsibility for making the policies work. We hope that in the media there will be a positive emphasis on solutions and not just a reporting of tragedies. Local as well as national media have a part to play. DATs may wish to assist in media briefings on how the prevention of drug-related deaths is being tackled.

AWARENESS TO EMBRACE BOTH ACUTE DRUG-RELATED DEATHS AND THOSE RESULTING FROM CHRONIC ILLNESSES.

10.7   Heightened awareness is needed in both these sectors of concern and neither should be the enemy of the other. But we believe it is at present particularly the threat from virus diseases which is being underestimated.

A HEIGHTENED LEVEL OF KNOWLEDGE AND COMMITMENT AND AN ATTITUDINAL SHIFT ACROSS ALL RELEVANT AGENCIES

10.8   We are suggesting that a fundamentally important contribution to the success of policy will be made by the knowledge, commitment and attitudes of agencies and every individual who works within them. Preventing drug-related deaths should be much higher on their agendas than has sometimes previously been the case. It should be core business with complacency unacceptable and a true sense of urgency. What we are calling for here is a change in culture.

MULTIPLE IMPROVEMENT IN RELEVANT PRACTICES ACROSS AGENCIES AND AUDIT OF PERFORMANCE

10.9   The details of the work which now needs to be addressed is covered at many earlier points in this report, and we believe that there are ample and rewarding opportunities for every agency to improve practice. We believe that audit here not only implies the pro-active review of particular facets of agency policy and the collection of appropriate data, but also a willingness in open and constructive fashion to examine in detail the circumstances surrounding the death of any current or recently discharged client.

AGENCY PRACTICES TO BE AIMED STRONGLY AND PERSISTENTLY AT REDUCTION IN INJECTED DRUG USE

10.10 We have highlighted the crucial importance of reduction in the prevalence of injection both for the prevention of deaths from immediate causes, and also for those which result from chronic virus diseases. Teaching and facilitating safer injection may often be a sensible intermediate goal. But to prevent drug-related deaths on a significant scale, that goal must be seen as only intermediate. The further and urgent goal must be to get individuals away from a practice which, on all the evidence now available, carries high risks which cannot at all certainly be obviated by harm minimisation strategies.

AN END TO LAX AND IRRSEPONSIBLE PRESCRIBING AND A RADICAL CURTAILMENT OF METHADONE-RELATED DEATHS.

10.11 It is deeply unsatisfactory that while energy and resources are aimed in one sector of activity at reduction in drug-related deaths, practices should be allowed to continue elsewhere which flagrantly risk increase in deaths. We refer here to the lax system which permits the prescribing and dispensing of methadone so that it spills to the illicit market, the too generous prescribing of benzodiazepines, and the continued prescribing of tablets of any drug which can be injected, and the prescribing of ampoules. Deaths due to methadone may fairly today be described as a cause for national reproach : they should not be happening and they should be prevented from happening. No overall policy can here have credibility if these prescribing abuses are allowed to continue. Preventing medically caused drug-related deaths must be an essential and urgent element of the policy frame. Prescribers must acknowledge a responsibility toward their communities, as well as toward the individual drug user.

A STRENGTHENED RESPONSE TO DRUG MISUSE BY THE PRISON SERVICE

10.12 We see recent developments in the prison service response to drug misuse as promising. If the prisons fail adequately to deal with drug issues, a vital element in the overall strategies to prevent drug-related deaths will be missing

BETTER LIAISON BETWEEN AGENCIES

10.13 The need for better liaison between different types of agency has become apparent at several points in this report. For instance, the more adequate care and after-care of prisoners who have drug problems will require collaboration between prison staff and specialist drug services. Specialist drug services will often need better access to advice from experts in virus diseases. The survival of patients who present with dual diagnosis of drug misuse and psychiatric illness, may depend on strengthened liaison between the two types of service. Drug treatment agencies may need input from agencies which have special experience with the treatment of drinking problems. Dealing more energetically with alcohol will help prevent drug-related deaths.

ENHANCED INVESTMENT IN PROFESSIONAL TRAINING

10.14 A great deal which has been said in this report points to the salient contribution which enhanced professional and interdisciplinary training must be expected to make to the policy frame. We suspect that the knowledge, skills, and attitudes needed to prevent drug-related deaths are at present often under-represented in teaching programmes, in the agendas of professional meetings, and in the teaching texts. An educational and training initiative will therefore be intrinsic to the overall policy initiative.

THE NEED TO TARGET SOCIAL DEPRIVATION

10.15 The rate of premature deaths among drug misusers is strongly and positively related to social deprivation. Poverty and social disadvantage carry with them increased rates of injected drug use, and lifestyles which may perhaps also increase the riskiness of use while decreasing access to care. Any measures which deal successfully with social exclusion are therefore likely to reduce the toll of drug-related deaths and we see action on exclusion as making a vital background contribution to the policy mix which we recommend.

ATTEMPTS ARE NEEDED ACTIVELY TO INVOLVE DRUG USERS THEMSELVES IN RESPONSIBILITY FOR REDUCING DRUG-RELATED DEATHS

10.16 Drug policies could perhaps sometimes be faulted for giving the impression that their latent assumption is that drug misusers constitute the problem but can never be expected to take an active hand in its solution. Policies to prevent drug-related deaths must more often in the future take drug users into partnership. They need information as much as the professionals, and they should share in determining what information is required and in what form. We believe that the message that drug users have a personal responsibility to avoid overdose and virus infection or risking the lives of their partners or friends, would be a useful corrective to the assumption that they are incapable of exercising responsibility. That message of self-responsibility would, in our view, be empowering.

A MORE DETERMINED ATTEMPT TO REACH DRUG USERS WHO ARE OUTSIDE AGENCY CONTACT

10.17 Many deaths from overdose occur among drug users who are not in contact with agencies and as we noted in Chapter 8, about 60% of injecting users are hepatitis C positive by the time they first turn to an agency for help. Policies directed solely at people who are currently enrolled with agencies, will therefore only reach a small part of the total target population. Health messages should be got to the totality of that population.

RESPONSE TO THE NEEDS OF FAMILIES

10.18   An inquest may at times help with the grief and perplexity of bereaved families and friends. Otherwise we believe that far too little thought has been given to how such people can be helped, and we feel that the issue should be addressed at local level. Families may also have a role in helping prevent drug-related deaths.

A CRUCIAL ROLE FOR DATS AND DAATS

10.19   We could not envisage the recommendations we propose in this report achieving their intention without the support of DATs and DAATs. They alone have the capacity to foster and facilitate the multi-sectoral and inter-sectoral activity which together constitute the needed initiatives for every locality.

BETTER INVESTMENT IN RESEARCH WHICH CAN HELP PREVENT DRUG-RELATED DEATHS.

10.20   We urge a review of the adequacy of current research in this area. Some interesting research has been conducted, and it has helped in the preparation of this report. Some gaps in knowledge have been identified in this report (for example see paragraphs 2.32, 3.4, 3.15, 7.21, and 9.3), but we have no sense at present of a strategic plan in place which can match future research activity to policy needs relating to prevention of drug-related deaths. We are aware that there are financial constraints across the board for research on drug misuse. The successful implementation of a planned and intentional research initiative to support prevention of drug-related deaths could, however, provide an interesting test case for how the research and policy connection in the drugs arena can be better planned and better handled.

CAUSES FOR OPTIMISM

10.21   This report deals with a worrying problem and at present that problem is evidently year by year getting worse. We are not afraid to say that the challenge set by this problem is intrinsically difficult. Up to now it has in our view too often been neglected or shrugged aside with complacency.

10.22   At the end of the exercise which underlies this report and having listened to, and read evidence from many informed people, we are in no mood for facile optimism. That said, we want to express a conjoint view based on objective consideration of the problem, identification of the many opportunities open for fruitful action, and our sense of the strengths of what is now a very experienced field. That view is that drug-related deaths can, will and must in the near future be radically reduced in number.

APPENDIX A

PREVENTION WORKING GROUP

Members including co-opted members

Professor G Edwards, Institute of Psychiatry, Addiction Research Unit, London

Mrs J Barlow, Independent consultant and researcher, Peebleshire

Ms J Christian, Druglink, North Staffs

Dr W Clee, General Practitioner, Near Cardiff

Dr L Gruer, Greater Glasgow Health Board

Professor J Henry, St Mary's Hospital, London

Mr T Herbert, Independent consultant and counsellor for drug and alcohol problems, Nottingham

Mr R Howard, Drugscope, London

Mr R Ives, Independent consultant on young people and drugs, London

Ms R Joyce, Drugscope, London

Mr J Kay, Healthwise, Liverpool

Professor N McKeganey, Centre for Drug Misuse Research, Glasgow University

Professor G Pearson, Department of Community Studies, Goldsmiths College, London

Mr A Ramsey, Scotland Against Drugs, Glasgow

Dr R Robertson, General Practitioner, Edinburgh

Professor J Strang, National Addiction Centre, London

Dr D Temple, WCPGPE, Cardiff University

Dr C Tibbs, St George's, Hospital, London

Inspector P Wotton, Metropolitan Police, London

Secretary: Mr R Rhodes (to July 1999)
            Mr S Hewett

Assistant Secretary: Miss J Wright

Assisted by: Miss F Pembroke

Officials:

Home Office
Mr V Hogg
Mr J Corkery
Mr R Clifford

Scottish Executive
Mrs M Cuthbert

Northern Ireland Office
Dr W B Smith

Department of Health
Mr T Thake

Welsh Drug and Alcohol Unit
Ms C Weatherup

Welsh Assembly
Mr D Robinson

Uk Anti-Drugs Co-ordination Unit
Mr J Critchley

Department for Education and Employment
Mr J Ford

APPENDIX B

ACKNOWLEDGEMENTS

The Working Group is grateful to the following who gave presentations:

Ms O Christophersen, The Office of National Statistics

Ms S Kelly, The Office of National Statistics.

Mr M Burgess, The Coroners' Society

Mr M Blank, Surrey Alcohol and Drug Advisory Service

Dr C Luke, Royal Liverpool Hospital

Professor L Appleby, Manchester University

Ms C Clancy, St George's Hospital Medical School

Dr Oyefeso, St George's Hospital Medical School

Dr E Finch, Institute of Psychiatry

Dr P Fineron, University of Edinburgh

Dr S Gore, Medical Research Council

Dr P Knapman, Westminster Coroner's Court

Dr I Hill, Guy's Hospital

Dr M Starck, St George's Hospital Medical School

APPENDIX C

Coroner's certificate after inquest (Form 99(REV) A&B - white)

CORONER'S CERTIFICATE AFTER INQUEST furnished under section 11(7) of the Coroner's Act 1988	To be completed by Registrar
	Register No
	Entry No

To the _____ Registrar of Births and Deaths

Inquest held on
at
Was a post-mortem held?

PART I   PARTICULARS OF DECEASED (Not still born - see separate Form 99A)

1. Date and place of death

2. Name and surname   3. Sex

                                                     4. Maiden surname of woman who has married

5. Date and place of birth

6. Occupation and usual address

Cause of death   I(a)
                   (b)
                   (c)
                   II
                   Verdict

PART II   VISITING FORCES
The inquest was adjourned on   { *under section 7 of the Visiting Forces Act 1952
                                     *and has not been resumed.

PART III   BURIAL/CREMATION   †Enter Order for Burial/Certificate E for Cremation
I have issued †
           on
           to
           of

PART IV   MARITAL CONDITION etc.   All persons aged 16 and over
Insert appropriate number in box. 1.Single 2.Married 3.Widowed 4..Divorced 5. Not Known

	Day	Month	Year
If married enter date of birth of surviving spouse			

I certify that the findings of the inquest were as above.

Date   Signed

Name

Appointment

Jurisdiction

* Delete as necessary

	To be completed by Registrar	
Name and surname of deceased	District & SD Nos	
	Register No	
	Entry No	

PART V ACCIDENT OR MISDADVENTURE (including deaths from neglect or from anaesthetics)

1. Place where accident occurred †

0.	Home	5.	Street or highway
1.	Farm	6.	Public building
2.	Mine or quarry	7.	Resident institution
3.	Industrial place or premises	8.	Other specified place
4.	Place of recreation or sport	9.	Place not known

2. To be completed for all persons aged 16 and over
    When injury was received deceased was †

1. On way to, or from work
2. At work
3. Elsewhere

3. Details of how accident happened:

4. If motor vehicle incident, deceased was †

0.	Driver of motor vehicle other than motor cycle	5.	Rider of animal, occupant of animal-drawn vehicle
1.	Passenger in motor vehicle other than motor cycle	6.	Pedal cyclist
2.	Motor cyclist	7.	Pedestrian
3.	Passenger on motor cycle	8.	Other specified person
4.	Occupant of tram car	9.	Not known

5. Interval between injury and death †   †

1. Less than one year   2. One year or more

† Please insert approximate number in box

APPENDIX D

REFERENCES

Chapter 2

1.   Merigian K. & Blaho K. (1995) The role of pharmacology and forensics in the death of an asthmatic. *Journal of Analytical Toxicology* 19(6), 522-8.

2.   Benowitz N.L. (1992) How toxic is cocaine? *Ciba-Foundation-Symposia* 166, 125-43.

3.   Spivey WH, Euerle B. (1990) Neurologic complications of cocaine abuse. *Annals of Emergency Medicine* 19, 1422-28.

4.   Henry JA, Jeffreys KJ, & Dawling S. (1992) Toxicity and deaths from 3, 4-methylenedioxymeth-amphetamine ("ecstasy") *Lancet* 340(8816), 384-387.

5.   Burke A.P., Kalva P., Li L., Smialek J. & Vermani R. (1997) Infectious endocarditis & sudden unexpected death. *Journal of Heart Valve Disease* 6(2), 198-203.

6.   Krausz M., Degkwitz P., Haasen C. & Verthein U. (1996) Opioid addiction & suicidality. *Crisis* 17, 175-81.

7.   Hammersley, R., Cassidy, M.T. & Oliver, J. (1995) Drugs associated with drug-related deaths in Edinburgh and Glasgow, November 1990 to October 1992, *Addiction* 90, 959-965.

8.   Hall, W.D. (1996) How can we reduce heroin overdose death. *Medical Journal of Australia* 164, 197-198.

9.   Harding-Pink D. (1990) Mortality following release from prison. *Medicine, Science and Law* 30(1), 12-16.

10. Shewan, D., Hammersley, R., Oliver, J. & Macpherson, S. (1996) *Death by drug overdose among female drug injectors from Strathclyde recently released from prison* (Edinburgh, Chief Scientists Office).

11. Seaman, S.R., Brettle, R.P. & Gore, S.M. (1998) Mortality from overdose among injecting drug users recently released from prison: database linkage study, *British Medical Journal* 316, 426-428.

12. Rajs, J. & Fugelstad, A. (1994) *Narcotics-related deaths in Stockholm 1986-1993* (Stockholm, Department of Forensic Medicine, Stockholm Psychiatric Dependency Clinic, St Gorans Hospital, Stockholm).

13. Ingold, F.R. (1986) Study of deaths related to drug abuse in France and Europe, *Bulletin of Narcotics* 38, 81-89.

14. Davoli, M., Perucci, D., Forastiere, F., Doyle, P et al (1993) Risk Factors for Overdose Mortality: A Case -control Study within a Cohort of Intravenous Drug Users. *International Journal of Epidemiology* 22, 273-277.

15. Roberts, I., Barker, M. & Li, L. (1997) Analysis of trends in deaths from accidental drug poisoning in teenagers, 1985-95, *British Medical Journal* 315, 289.

16. Oppenheimer, E., Tobutt, C., Taylor, C. & Andrew, T. (1994) Death and survival in a cohort of heroin addicts from London clinics: a 22-year follow-up study, *Addiction* 89, 1299-1308.

17. Esklid, A., Magnus, P., Samuelsen, S.O., Sohlberg, C. & Kittelsen, P. (1993) Differences in mortality rates and causes of death between HIV-positive and HIV-negative intravenous drug users, *International Journal of Epidemiology*, 22(1), 315-320.

18. Goddop, M., Griffiths, P., Powis, B., Williamson, S. & Strang, J. (1996) Frequency of nonfatal heroin overdose - Survey of heroin users recruited in non-clinical settings, *British Medical Journal* 313, 402-402.

19. Taylor, A., Frischer, M. & Goldberg, D. (1996) Non-fatal overdosing is related to polydrug use in Glasgow, *British Medical Journal* 313, 1400-1401.

20. Edston E. & Hage-Hamsten M. (1997) Anaphylactoid Shock, a common cause of death in heroin addicts. *Allergy* 52, 950-4.

21. Wolters et al. (1982) *Lancet* ii, 1233-7.

22. Department of Transportation. National Transportation Safety Board report, Washington DC, Feb 5 1990.

23. Williams AG, Peat MA, Crouch DJ et al. (1985) Drugs in fatally injured young male drivers. Public Health Report 100, 19-25.

24. Andreasson S. & Allebeck P. (1990) Cannabis & mortality among young men. *Scandinavian Journal of Social Medicine* 18(1): 9-15.

25. Cregler L.L. (1991) Cocaine: the newest risk factor for cardiovascular disease, *Clinical Cardiology* 14, 449-456.

26. Coniglio K. (1991) Cocaine-induced acute myocardial infarction. *Critical Care Nurse.* 11, 16-25.

27. Goldfrank L.R. & Hoffman R.S. (1991) The cardiovascular effects of cocaine. *Annals of Emergency Medicine* 20, 165-175.

28. Isner J.M., Chokshi S.K. (1991) Cardiac complications of cocaine abuse. *Annual Review of Medicine* 42, 133-8.

29. Perper J.A. & van Theil D.H. (1992) Cardiovascular complications of cocaine abuse. *Recent Developments in Alcoholism* 10, 343-61.

30. Virmani R. (1991) Cocaine-associated cardiovascular disease: clinical and pathological aspects. *NIDA Research Monograph* 108, 220-9.

31. Fessler R.D., Esshaki C.M., Stankewitz R.C., Johnson R.R. & Diaz F.G. (1997) The neurovascular complications of cocaine. *Surgical Neurology* 47(4), 339-45.

32. Herning R.I., King D.E., Better W. & Cadet J.L. (1997) Cocaine dependence: a clinical syndrome requiring neuroprotection. *Annals of the New York Academy of Sciences* 825, 323-327.

33. Volkow N.D., Mullani N., Gould K.L., Adler S. & Krajewski K. (1988) Cerebral blood flow in chronic cocaine users. A study with positron emission tomography. *British Journal of Psychiatry* 152, 641-6481.

34. Marzuk P.M., Tardiff K., Leon A.C., Hirsch C.S., Portera L., Iqbal M.I., Nock M.K. & Hartwell N. (1998) Ambient temperature and mortality from unintentional cocaine overdose. *JAMA* 279, 1795-800.

35. Pottieger, A.E., Tressell, P.A., Inciardi, J.A., Rosales, T.A. (1992). Cocaine use patterns and overdose. *Journal of Psychoactive Drugs* 24, 399-410.

36. Tardiff K, Marzuk P.M., Leon, A.C., Portera, L., Hartwell, N., Hirsch, C.S and Stajic, M. (1996) Accidental fatal drug overdoses in New York City 1990-1992 *American Journal of Drug and Alcohol Abuse* 22, 135-146.

37. Milroy C.M., Clark J.C., Forrest A.R.W. (1996) Pathology of deaths associated with "ecstasy" and "eve" misuse. *Journal of Clinical Pathology* 49, 149-153.

38. Harries D.P., De Silva R. (1992) Ecstasy and intracerebral haemorrhage. *Scottish Medical Journal* 37, 150-52.

39. Hooft, P.J. & Vandevoorde, H.P. (1994) Reckless behavior related to the use of 3, 4-methylenedioxymethamphetamine (Ecstasy) - Apropos of a fatal accident during car-surfing, *International Journal of Legal Medicine* 106, 328-329.

40. Crifasi, J. & Long, C. (1996) Traffic fatality related to the use of methylenedioxymethamphetamine, *Journal of Forensic Sciences*, 41, 1082-1084.

41. Volatile Substance Abuse: A Report by the Advisory Council on the Misuse of Drugs. HMSO 1995 ISBN 0-11-341141-3

42. Taylor, J.C., Norman, C.L., Bland, J.M., Ramsey, J.D. & Anderson, H.R. (1998) *Trends in Deaths Associated with Abuse of Volatile Substances 1971-1996* (London, Department of Public Health Sciences and the Toxicology Unit Department of Cardiological Sciences, St George's Hospital Medical School, Cranmer Tarrace, London).

43. Zador, D., Sunjic, S. & Darke, S. (1996) Heroin-related deaths in New-South-Wales, 1992 - toxicological findings and circumstances, *Medical Journal of Australia*, 164, 204-207.

44. O'Doherty, M. & Farrington, A. (1997) Estimating local opioid addict mortality. *Addiction Research*, 4, 321-327.

45. Frisher, M., Bloor, M., Goldberg, D. *et al.* (1993) Mortality among injecting drug users: a critical reappraisal, *Journal of Epidemiology and Community Health*, 47, 59-63.

Chapter 3

1. Prior, P (1989) The Social Organisation of Death: Medical Discourse and Social Practices in Belfast. London, Macmillan.

2. Ghodse, H., Clancy C., Oyefeso, A., Goldfinch, R., Pollard M., Corkery J (1998) Drug -related deaths as reported by Coroners in England and Wales. National Programme on Substance Abuse Deaths Report 1, April 1998.

3. Taylor, J.C., Norman, C.L., Bland, J.M., Ramsey, J.D. & Anderson, H.R. (1998) *Trends in Deaths Associated with Abuse of Volatile Substances 1971-1996* (London, Department of Cardiological Sciences, St George's Hospital Medical School, Cranmer Terrace, London).

4. O'Doherty, M. & Farrington, A. (1997) Estimating local opioid addict mortality, *Addiction Research*, 4, 321-327.

5. Frischer, M., Bloor, M., Goldberg, D. *et al.* (1993) Mortality among injecting drug users: a critical reappraisal, *Journal of Epidemiology and Community Health*, 47, 59-63.

6. Oppenheimer, E., Tobutt, C., Taylor, C. & Andrew, T. (1994) Death and survival in a cohort of heroin addicts from London clinics: a 22-year follow-up study, *Addiction* 89, 1299-1308.

7. Esmail, A., Meyer, L., Pottier, A. & Wright, S. (1993) Deaths from volatile substance-abuse in those under 18 years - results from a national epidemiologic-study, *Archives Of Disease In Childhood* 69, 356-360.

8. Ghodse, A.H., Sheehan, M., Taylor, C. & Edwards, G. (1985) Deaths of drug-addicts in the United-Kingdom 1967-81, *British Medical Journal* 290, 425-428.

9. Bentley, A.J. & Busuttil, A. (1996) Deaths among drug-abusers in south-east Scotland (1989-1994), *Medicine, Science And The Law* 36, 231-236.

10. Cassidy, M.T., Curtis, M., Muir, G. & Oliver, J.S. (1995) Drug-abuse deaths in Glasgow in 1992 - a retrospective study. *Medicine, Science And The Law* 35, 207-212.

11. Esmail, A., Warburton, B., Bland, J.M., Anderson, H.R. & Ramsey, J. (1997) Regional variations in deaths from volatile solvent abuse in Great Britain, *Addiction* 92, 1765-1771.

12. Harlow, K.C. (1990) Patterns of rates of mortality from narcotics and cocaine overdose in Texas, 1976-87, *Public Health Reports* 105, 455-462.

13. Kaa, E. (1992) Drug-abuse in western Denmark during the eighties. Fatal poisonings among drug-abusers, *Forensic Science International* 55, 75-82.

14.   Borrell, C., Plasencia, A., Pasarin, I. & Ortun, V. (1997) Widening social inequalities in mortality: the case of Barcelona, a southern European city, *Journal of Epidemiology and Community Health* 51, 659-667.

15.   Crighton, D. & Towl, G. (1997) Suicides in prison in England and Wales 1988-95; psychiatric history and drug abuse, *Prison Service Journal*, 44-47.

16.   Sherr, L. (1995) Suicide and AIDS: lessons from a case note audit in London, *AIDS Care - Psychological and Socio-Medical Aspects of AIDS/HIV* 7, 109-116.

17.   Catalan, J. & Pugh, K. (1995) Suicidal behaviour and HIB infection - is there a link? *AIDS Care - Psychological and Socio-Medical Aspects of AIDS/HIV* 7, 117-121.

18.   Carvajal, M.J., Vicioso, C., Santamaria, J.M. & Bosco, A. (1995) AIDS and suicide issues in Spain, *AIDS Care - Psychological and Socio-Medical Aspects of AIDS/HIV* 7, 135-138.

19.   Deykin, E.Y. & Buka, S.L. (1994) Suicidal ideation and attempts among chemically dependent adolescents, *American Journal of Public Health* 84, 634-639.

20.   Chatham, L.R., Knight, K., Joe, G.W. & Simpson, D.D. (1995) Suicidality in a sample of methadone maintenance clients, *American Journal of Drug and Alcohol Abuse* 21, 345-361.

21.   ACMD (1995) Volatile Substance Abuse: A Report by the Advisory Council on the Misuse of Drugs. HMSO (1995) ISBN 0-11-341141-3.

22.   Fischer, B. (1995) Drugs, communities, and 'harm reduction' in Germany: the new relevance of 'public health' prinicples in local repsonses, *Journal of Public Health Policy* 16, 389-411.

23.   Ingold, F.R. (1986) Study of deaths related to drug abuse in France and Europe, *Bulletin of Narcotics* 38, 81-89.

24.   Gutierrez-Cebollada, J., de la Torre, R., Ortuno, J., Garces, J.M. & Cami, J. (1994) Psychotropic-drug consumption and other factors associated with heroin overdose, *Drug and Alcohol Dependence* 35, 169-174.

25.   Hyatt, R.R. & Rhodes, W. (1995) The price and purity of cocaine - the relationship to emergency room visits and death, and to drug-use among arrestees, *Statistics In Medicine* 14, 655-668.

26.   Howard, D.J. (1984) Drug-related deaths in a major metropolitan area: a sixteen year review, *The Journal of Applied Social Sciences* 8, 235-248.

27.   Darke, S and Ross, J. (1997) Overdose Risk Perceptions and Behaviours among Heroin Users in Sydney Australia *European Addiction* Research 3(2), 87-92.

28.   Rhodes, T. (1995) Theorizing and researching 'risk': notes on the social relations of risk ini heroin users' lifestyles, in: Aggleton, P., Davies, P. & Hart, G. (eds) *AIDS: Safety, Sexuality and Risk*, pp. 125-171 (London, Taylor and Francis).

29.   Rhodes, T. (1997) Risk theory in epidemic times: Sex, drugs and the social organisation of 'risk behaviour', *Sociology of Health & Illness* 19, 208-227.

30.   Darke S., Ross, J., Hall, W. (1996) Overdose among Heroin Users in Sydney Australia: Responses to Overdose *Addiction* 3, 413-417.

31.   Zador, D., Sunjic, S. & Darke, S. (1996) Heroin-related deaths in New-South-Wales, 1992 - toxicological findings and circumstances, *Medical Journal of Australia* 164, 204-207.

32.   Walsh R. (1991) Opioid Drug Accidental Deaths in Newcastle Area of New South Wales 1970-1987 *Drug and Alcohol Review* 10, 79-83.

33.   Manning. F., Ingraham L. (1983) Drug Overdose among US Soldiers in Europe 1978-1979 Demographics and Toxicology *International Journal of Addictions* 18, 153-156.

34.   Garriot, J., Sturner, W. (1973) Morphine concentrations and survival periods in acute heroin fatalities *Journal of Analytical Toxicology* 18, 22-28.

35. Nakamura, G. (1978) Toxicological assessments in acute heroin fatalities *Clinical Toxicology* 13, 75-87.

36. Darke S., Ross, J. (1997) Overdose Rosk Perceptions and Behaviours among Heroin users in Sydney Australia *European Addiction Research* 3, 87-92.

Chapter 4

1. WHO (1977): *International Classification of Diseases: Manual of the International Statistical Classification of Diseases, Injuries, and Causes of Death (Ninth Revision, 1975)*. Geneva: World Health Organisation.

2. WHO (1992): *International Classification of Diseases: International Statistical Classification of Diseases and Related Health Problems (Tenth Revision)*. Geneva: World Health Organisation.

3. Arrundale, J and Cole, K. (1995). *Collection of information on drug-related deaths by the General Register Office for Scotland*. Edinburgh: Vital Events Branch, General Register Office for Scotland.

4. Corkery, J.M. (1997) *Statistics of drug addicts notified to the Home Office, United Kingdom, 1996*. Home Office Statistical Bulletin 22/1997. London: Home Office Research and Statistics Directorate.

5. Ghodse, H., Clancy, C., Oyefeso, A., Goldfinsch, R., Pollard, M. and Corkery, J. (1998b). *Drug-related Deaths as reported by Coroners in England and Wales: July – December, 1997*. London: Centre for Addiction Studies, St George's Hospital Medical School.

6. Ghodse, H., Clancy, C., Oyefeso, A., Goldfinch, R., Pollard, M. and Corkery, J. (1999a). *Drug-related Deaths as reported by Coroners in England and Wales: January – June, 1998*. London: Centre for Addiction Studies, St George's Hospital Medical School.

7. Ghodse, H., Clancy, C., Oyefeso, A., Goldfinch, R., Pollard, M. and Corkery, J. (1999b). *Drug-related Deaths as reported by Coroners in England and Wales: July – December, 1998*. London: Centre for Addiction Studies, St George's Hospital Medical School.

8. DETR (Department of the Environment, Transport and the Regions). (1998). Press Notice 94/ Transport 11 February 1998 "Government acts on drug-driving enforcement".

9. Danish National Board of Health (1997). *Drug-related death in Europe – Quality and Comparability of data on drug-related deaths*. Final report of the Working Group for Subtask 3.3 of the EMCDDA Programme 1996/97.

10. EMCDDA. (1999) *Feasibility of implementing standards for collecting data of drug-related deaths in EU Member States: results of the questionnaire Drug-Related Deaths*. Lisbon: European Monitoring Centre on Drugs and Drug Addiction.

Chapter 5

1. UKACDU (United Kingdom Anti-Drugs Co-ordination Unit). (1999). First Annual report and National Plan. London: Cabinet Office.

Chapter 7

1. Sheridan, J., Strang, J., Barber, N. and Glanz, A. (1996). Role of community pharmacies in relation to HIV prevention and drug misuse: findings from the 1995 National Survey in England and Wales. *British Medical Journal* 313, 272-274.

2. Hall, W., Lynskey, M., Degenhardt, L. (1998). Trends in methadone-related deaths in the United Kingdom 1985-1995.

3. Drug Misuse and Dependence – Guidelines on clinical management. The Stationery Office (1999). ISBN 0-11-322277-7.

4. Clark, J.C., Milroy, C.M. and Forrest, A.R.W. (1995). Deaths from methadone use. *Annuls of Clinical Forensic Medicine* 2, 143-144.

5. Cairns, A., Robers, I.S.D. and Benbow, E.W. (1996). Characteristics of fatal methadone overdose in Manchester, 1985-1994. *British Medical Journal* 313, 246-265.

6. Obafunwa, J., & Busuttil, A. (1994). Deaths from substance overdose in the Lothian and Borders Region of Scotland (1983-1991) *Human and Experimental Toxicology* 13, 401-406.

7. Bentley, A. and Brusuttil, A. (1996). Deaths among drug abusers in South-east Scotland (1989-1994). *Medical Science Law* 36(3), 231-236.

8. Hammersley, R., Cassidy, M. and Oliver, J. (1995). Drugs associated with drug-related deaths in Edinburgh and Glasgow, November 1990 to October 1992. *Addiction* 90, 959-865.

9. Cassidy, M., Curtis, M., Muir, G. and Oliver, J. (1995). Drug abuse deaths in Glasgow in 1992 – a retrospective study. *Medical Science Law* 35(3), 207-212.

10. Swensen, G. (1998). Opioid drug deaths in Western Australia: 1974-1984. *Australian Drug and Alcohol Review* 7, 181-185.

11. Williamson, P.A., Foreman, K.J., White, J.M. and Anderson, G. (1997). Methadone-related overdose deaths in South Australia, 1984-1994: How safe is prescribing? *Medical Journal of Australia* 166, 302-305.

12. Zador, D., Sunjic, S. and Basili, H. (1998). Deaths in Methadone Maintenance Treatment in New South Wales, 1990-1995. In W. Hall (Ed), *Proceedings of An International Opioid Overdose Symposium.* National Drug and Alcohol Research Centre Monograph Number 35. Sydney: National Drug and Alcohol Research Centre.

13. Caplehorn, J.R.M. (1998). Deaths in the first two weeks of methadone treatment in NSW in 1994: Identifying cases of iatrogenic methadone toxicity. *Drug and Alcohol Review* 17, 9-17.

14. Chabalko, J., LaRosa, J., and DuPont, R. (1973). Death of methadone users in the District of Columbia. *The International Journal of the Addictions* 8(6), 897-908.

15. Greene, M., Luke J., & Dupont, R. (1974a). Opiate Overdose deaths in the District of Colombia. Part II-Methadone related fatalities. *Journal of Forensic Sciences* 19, 575-584.

16. Green, M., Brown, B., and DuPont, R. (1975). Controlling the abuse of illicit methadone in Washington, DC. *Archives of General Psychiatry* 32, 221-226.

17. Barrett, D., Luk, A., Parrish, R., and Jones, T. (1996). An investigation of medical examiner cases in which methadone was detected, Harris County, Texas, 1987-1992. *Journal of Forensic Sciences* 41(3), 442-448.

18. Alexander, B.K., MacInnes, T.M., and Beyerstein, B.L. (1998). Methadone and mortality among drug users. *British Columbia Medical Journal* 30(3), 160-163.

19. Editor Kathleen Parfitt. (1999). Martindale: the complete drug reference 32nd edition. *Pharmaceutical Press London, p55.*

20. Ward S, Marrick R.P., and Hall W eds. (1998) *Methadone Maintenance Treatment and other Opioid Replacement Therapies.* Amsterdam, Harwood Academic Publishers.

21. Marsh L.A. (1998) The efficacy of methadone maintenance interventions in reducing illicit opiate use, HIV risk behaviour and criminality: a meta-analysis. *Addiction* 93, 505-514.

22. Ward, J., Marrick, R.P., and Hall, W. (1992). *Key issues in methadone maintenance treatment.* Sydney: New South Wales University Press.

23. Ball. J.C. and Ross, A. (1991). *The Effectiveness of Methadone Maintenance Treatment: Patients, programs, services, and outcomes.* New York: Springer.

24. Ball, J.C., Lange, W.R., Myers, C.P., and Friedman, S.R. (1998). Reducing the risk of AIDS through methadone maintenance treatment. *Journal of Health and Social Behaviour* 29, 214-226.

25. Darke, S., Hall, W., and Carless, J. (1990). Drug use, injecting practices and sexual behaviour of opioid users in Sydney, Australia. *British Journal of Addiction* 85, 1603-1609.

26. Darke, S., Hall, W., Heather, N., Ward, J., and Wodak, A. (1991). The reliability and validity of a scale to measure HIV risk-taking behaviour among intravenous drug users. *AIDS* 5, 181-185.

27. Abdul-Quader, A.S., Friedman, S.R., Des Jarlais, D., Marmor, M.M., Maslansky, R., and Bartelme, S. (1987). Methadone maintenance and behaviour by intravenous drug users that can transmit HIV. *Contemporary Drug Problems* 14, 425-434.

28. Schoenbaum, E.E., Hartel, D., Selwyn, P.A., Klein, R.S., Davenny, K., Rogers, M., Feiner, C., and Friedland, G. (1989). Risk factors for human immunodeficiency virus infection in intravenous drug users. *New England Journal of Medicine* 321, 874-879.

29. Novick, D.M., Joseph, H., Croxson, T.S., Salisitz, E.A., Wang, G., Richman, B.L., Poretsky, L., Keefe, J.B., and Whimbey, E. (1990). Abuse of antibody to human immunodeficiency virus in long-term, socially rehabilitated methadone maintenance patients. *Archives of Internal Medicine* 150, 97-99.

30. Blix, O. and Gronbladh, L. (1988). *AIDS and IV heroin addicts: The preventative effect of methadone maintenance in Sweden*. Paper presented to 4th International Conference on AIDS, Stockholm.

31. Metzger, D.S., Woody, G.E., MacLellan, A.T., O'Brien, C.P., Druley, P., Navaline, H., DePhilippis, D., Stolley, P. and Arbrutyn, E. (1993). Human Immunodeficiency Virus seroconversion among intravenous drug users in and out of treatment: An 18-month prospective follow-up. *Journal of Acquired Immune Deficiency syndrome*, 6, 1049-1055.

32. Moss, A.R., Vranizan, K., Gorter, R., Bacchetti, P., Watters, J. and Osmond, D. (1994). HIV seroconversion in intravenous drug users in San Francisco 1985-1990. *AIDS* 8, 223-231.

33. Caplehorn, J.R.M., Dalton, S.Y.N., Halder, F., Petrenas, A.M., and Nisbet, J.G. (1996). Methadone maintenance and addicts' risk of fatal heroin overdose. *Substance use and misuse* 31(2), 177-196.

34. Caplehorn, J.R.M., Dalton, S.Y.N., Cluff, M.C., and Petrenas, A.M. (1994). Retention in methadone maintenance and heroin addicts' risk of death. *Addiction* 89, 203-207.

35. Gearing, F.R., and Schweitzer, M.D. (1974). An epidemiologic evaluation of long-term methasone maintenance treatment for heroin addiction. *American Journal of Epidemiology* 100, 101-112.

36. Hall, W., Bell, J. and Carrels (1993). The history of criminal convictions among applicants for and Australian methadone maintenance program. *Drug and Alcohol Dependence*, 1993 (31), 123-129.

37. Maher, L., Dixon, D., Lynskey, M. and Hall, W. (1998). Running the risks: heroin, health and harm in South West Sydney. National Drug and Alcohol Research Centre, Sydney.

38. Hall, W. (1996). Methadone maintenance treatment as a crime control measure. *Contemporary Issues in Crime and Justice* 29, 1-12.

39. Brecher, E.M. (1972). *Licit and Illicit Drugs*. Boston: Little Brown Company.

40. Darke, S., Zador, D., and Sunjic, S. (1997). *Toxicological findings and circumstances of heroin-related deaths in South Western Sydney, 1995*. National Drug and Alcohol Reserch Centre Technical Report No. 40.

41. Darke, S., Zador, D. (1996). Fatal heroin overdose: A review. *Addiction* 91, 1757-1764.

42. Oppenheimer, E., Tobutt, C., Taylor, C. & Andrew, T. (1994). Death and survival in a cohort of heroin addicts from London clinics: A 22-year follow-up. *Addiction* 89, 1299-1308.

43. Zador, D., Sunjic, S., and Darke, S. (1996). Heroin-related deaths in New South Wales, 1992: Toxicological findings and circumstances. *Medical Journal of Australia* 164, 204-207.

44. Guttierrez-Cebollada, J., de la Torre, R., Ortunno, J., Garces, J. and Cami, J. (1994). Psychotropic drug consumption and other factors associated with heroin overdose, *Drug and Alcohol Dependence* 35, 169-174.

45. Ward, J., Bell, J., Mattick, R.P. and Hall, W. (1996). Methadone maintenance therapy for opioid dependence: A guide to appropriate use. *CNS Drugs* 6, 440-449.

46. Gruer L., Cooper G., Seymour A., Cassidy M., Oliver J. (1999) Methadone Deaths in Greater Glasgow and the rest of Stratclyde 1992-98 (unpublished).

47. ISD Scotland (1999) Drug Statistics Scotland 1998. Information and Statistics Division NHS in Scotland, Edinburgh.

48. Eissenberg, T., Bigelow, G., Stain, E.C., Walsh, S.L., Brooner, R.K., Stitzer, M.L. and Johnson, R.E. (1997) Dose-related efficacy of levo-alpha-acetyl-methadol (LAAM) for treatment of poioid dependence: A randomised clinical trial. Journal of the American Medical Association, 277, 1945-51.

49. Johnson, R.E., Eissenberg, T., Stitzer, M.L., Strain E.C., Liebson, L.A. and Bigelow, G.E. (1995) A placebo-controlled clinical trial of buprenorphine as a treatment for opioid dependence. Drug and Alcohol Dependence 40, 17-25.

Chapter 8

1. Burr A. 1983 Increased sales of opiates on the black market in the Piccadilly area. *British Medical Journal* 287, 883-885

2. Burr A. 1983 The Piccadilly Drug Scene. *British Journal of Addiction* 78, 5-19.

3. Bewley, T and Ghodse, A.H. 1983. The unacceptable face of private practice: prescription of controlled drugs to addicts. *British Medical Journal* 286, 1876-1877.

4. Foundation, J., Strang, J., Gossop, M., Farrell, M., Griffiths, P. (2000). Diversion of prescribed drugs by drug users in treatment: analysis of the UK market and new data from London. *Addiction* (in press).

5. Drug Misuse and Dependence – Guidelines on Clinical Management. The Stationery Office (1999). ISBN 0-11-322277-7.

6. Volatile Substance Abuse. A report by the Advisory Council on the Misuse of Drugs. HMSO (1995) ISBN 0-11-341141-3.

7. Taylor J.C., Norman C.L., Bland J.M., Ramsey J.D., Anderson H.R. Trends in Deaths Associated with Abuse of Volatile Substances 1971-1997. St George's Hospital Medical School.

8. Appleby L. (1999) Drug Misuse and Suicide: a tale of two services. *Addiction* 95(2), 175-177.

9. Working Party report: Services for Drug Misusers, (1998) *The Pharmaceutical Journal* 260, 418-423.

10. Strang S., Powis B., Best D., Vingow C., Griffiths P., Taylor C., Welch S. and Gossop M. (1999). Preventing overdose fatalities with take-home naloxone: pre-launch study of possible impact and acceptability. *Addiction* 94, 199-204.

11. Research Findings No. 70. Drug Testing Arrestees. Bennett T. Home Office Research and Statistics Directorate.

12. Drug Misusers and the Criminal Justice System. Part III Drug Misusers and the Prison System – An Integrated Approach. A report by the Advisory Council on the Misuse of Drugs. HMSO 1996. ISBN 0-11-341158-8

13. Drug Misusers and the Criminal Justice System. Part II Police, Drug Misusers and the Community. A report by the Advisory Council on the Misuse of Drugs. HMSO 1994. ISBN 0-11-341109-X.

14. Fairweather C., Skinner A. (1988). Women Offenders – a safer way. The Scottish Office. The Stationery Office Edinburgh.

15. Greater Glasgow Drug Action Team (2000) Fatal drug misuse-related overdoses in Greater Glasgow 1 January – 30 September 1999. Greater Glasgow Health Board.

16. DETR (Department of the Environment, Transport and the Regions). (1998). Press Notice 94/ Transport 11 February 1998 "Government acts on drug-driving enforcement".

Chapter 9

1. Coutinho R.A. (1998) HIV and hepatitis C among injecting drug users [editorial; comment]. *British Medical Journal* 317, 424-5.

2. Oxford Textbook of Medicine. 3rd edition, volume 2. Edited by Weatherall D.J., Leadingham J.G. and Warrell D.A. Oxford University Press 1996. pp2064-2069.

3. Diamantic I.D., Kouroumalis E., Koulentaki M., Fasler-Kan E., Schmid P.A., Hirsch HH. *et al.* (1997). Influence of hepatitis G virus infection on liver disease. *European Journal of Clinical Microbilogy of Infectious Diseases* 16, 916-9.

4. Cossart Y. (1998) TTV a common virus, but pathogenic? [comment]. *Lancet* 352, 164.

5. Gore S, personal communication.

6. Scottish Centre for Infection and Environmental Health (1999) SCIEH Weekly Report 33, 25-48.

7. AIDS and Drug Misuse Part 1. A report by the Advisory Council on the Misuse of Drugs. HMSO 1988. ISBN 0 11 321134 1.

8. AIDS and Drug Misuse Part 2. A report by the Advisory Council on the Misuse of Drugs. HMSO 1989. ISBN 0 11 321207 0.

9. AIDS and Drug Misuse Update. A report by the Advisory Council on the Misuse of Drugs 1993. ISBN 0-11-321631-9.

10. Stimson, G.V. (1996) Has the UK averted an epidemic of HIV infection among drug injectors? *Addiction* 91, 1085-1088.

11. Strang, J. (1998) Aids and Drug Misuse in the UK – Ten years on: achievements, failings and new harm reduction opportunities. Drugs: Education, Prevention and Policy 5, 293-304.

12. SCIEH weekly report: 26 January 1999. Scottish Centre for Infection and Environmental Health, Glasgow.

13. Majid A., Holmes R., Desselberger U., Simmonds P., McKee T.A. (1995) Molecular epidemiology of hepatitis C infection amongst intravenous drug users in rural communities. *Journal of Medical Virology* 46, 48-51.

14. Lamden K.H., Kennedy N., Beeching N.J., Lowe D., Morrison C.L., Mallinson H. *et al.* (1998) Hepatitis B and Hepatitis C virus infections: risk factors among drug users in Northwest England. *Journal of Infection.* 37, 260-9.

15. Goldberg D., Cameron S., McMenamin J. (1998) Hepatits C virus antibody prevalence among injecting drug users in Glasgow has fallen but remains high. *Communicable Diseases and Public Helath* 1, 95-7.

16. Gore S, personal communication.

17. Goldberg D., Taylor A., Hutchinson S., Cameron S. Scottish Centre for Infection and Environment health, unpublished data.

18. Hope et al (2000) forthcoming.

19. Alter M.J., Kruszon-Moran D., Nainan O.V., McQuillan G.M., Gao F., Moyer L.A. *et al.* (1999) The prevalence of hepatitis C virus infection in the United States, 1988 through 1994. *New England Journal of Medicine* 341, 556-62.

20. Alberti A., Chemello L., Benvegnu L. (1999) Natural history of hepatitis. *Clinical Journal of Hepatology* 31 (Suppl. 1), 17-24.

21. Poynard T., Marcellin P., Lee S.S., Niederau C., Minuk G.S., Ideo G. *et al.* (1998) Randomised trail of interferon alpha2b plus ribavirin for 48 weeks or for 24 weeks versus interferon alpha2b plus placebo for 48 weeks for treatment of chronic infection with hepatitis C virus. International Hepatitis Interventional Therapy Group (IHIT) [see comments]. *Lancet* 352, 1426-32.

22. Beasley R.P. (1998) Hepatitis B virus a major cause of hepatocellular carcinoma. *Cancer* 61, 1942-56.

23. Drug Misuse and Dependence – Guidelines on Clinical Management. The Stationery Office 1999. ISBN 0-11-322277-7.

24. Van Damme P., Kane M., Meheus A. (1997) Integration of hepatitis B vaccination into national immunisation programmes. Viral Hepatitis Prevention Board [see comments]. *British Medical Journal* 314, 1033-6.

25. Drug Misusers and the Criminal Justice System. Part III Drug Misusers and the Prison System – An Integrated Approach. A report by the Advisory Council on the Misuse of Drugs. HMSO 1996. ISBN 0-11-341158-8.

INDEX

Notes: Roman pagination refers to the preface; Decimal numbers refer to chapter numbers and paragraphs.

accident and emergency departments xxviii, 8.39, 8.41
accidental poisoning, teenagers 2.24
accidents xii, xiv, 8.1
  age 6.4
  alcohol 2.38
  cerebovascular 2.9–10, 2.33
  mental impairment 2.14
  methadone 7.12
  social deprivation 6.7–9
ACMD *see* Advisory Council on the Misuse of Drugs
action plan 8.25
acute illness xvii
acute poisoning xvii
administration routes xviii, 2.4
Advisory Council on the Misuse of Drugs (ACMD) xi
age xvi, 3.8–9
  trends 6.4
AIDS (Aquired Immune Deficiency Syndrome)
  data collection 4.44
  intravenous drug use 2.17
  Scotland xxx, 9.8
  statistics 1.3
  suicide xv, 3.13
alcohol
  data collection xvii, 4.6
  drug interactions xii, xiii, 1.11–12, 2.37–8, 2.43
  immediate death xv
  intravenous drug use 2.17
  recommendations 8.7
  toxicology 2.5
  wthdrawl 2.20
ambulance staff *see* emergency services
amphetamine sulphate
  pathology 2.9
  toxicity xv
  withdrawl 2.21
ampoules 8.13
anaphylactoid reactions 2.25
aneurysms xiv, 2.30
Anti-Drugs Co-ordinator 1.7
Arrundale, J. 4.33
atherosclerosis 2.30
availability xvi, 3.16
  methadone 7.8–10, 7.18

barbituates xv
  price 3.16
  toxicology 2.5
  withdrawl 2.20
Bentley, A.J. 3.8, 3.12
benzodiazepines xv, 2.35–6
  immediate death xxvi
  prescriptions xxvii
  price 3.16
  recommendations 8.7, 8.14–16
  Scotland xxiii
  toxicology 2.5
  as treatment 8.25
  withdrawl 2.21
body systems xiii
brain
  cerebrovascular accidents 2.9–10, 2.30
  dependence 2.20–1
  heroin xiv
buprenorphine (Temgesic) 2.27, 7.21
Busuttil, A.J. 3.8, 3.12

cannabis 2.28
  road traffic accidents 4.42
  toxicity xiv
CARAT *see* Counselling, Assessment, Referral and Advice and Treatment
cardiac arrhythmias 2.7, 2.29, 2.33
cardiac depression 2.7–8, 2.29
categorisation xxii–xxiii
causes of death
  data collection xxi
  ONS coding xix
  recommendations 4.24
  verdicts 4.14, 5.15
CDSC *see* Communicable Disease Surveillance Centre
central nervous system (CNS) 2.5
cerebrovascular accidents 2.9–10, 2.33
"chasing the dragon" 2.4
chemical structure 2.4
children, methadone poisoning xxiv
chronic illnesses xviii, xxx–xxxii, 9.1–39
circulatory disease xiii
  intravenous drug use 2.17
cirrhosis
  HCV 1.4, 9.21

cirrhosis—*contd*
  injected drugs xxxi, 2.37
clinical safety, methadone xxiv
cocaine 2.29–32
  see also crack cocaine
  immediate death xiv, xxvi
  kidney damage 2.12
  liver damage 2.11
  myocardial infarction 2.7
  police custody xxix
  price 3.16
  recommendations 8.7
  strokes 2.9
  withdrawl 2.21
Cole, K. 4.33
Communicable Disease Surveillance Centre
(CDSC) xx, 4.44–7
community liaisons xxix
comparative rates (Europe) xx, xxii
condoms
  cocaine smuggling 2.31
  HCV xxxi, 9.19
contaminants 2.4, 2.19
  anaphylactoid reactions 2.25
controlled drugs, prescriptions xxvii
coronary atheroma 2.29
coroners 4.11–19
  data collection xix-xx, 5.10
  notification xviii
  notification by doctors 4.9–10
  toxicological screening xxi
  training xxi
Coroners' Society of England and Wales xxi
counselling 8.9
Counselling, Assessment, Referral and Advice and
Treatment (CARAT) Scheme xxix, 8.52
crack cocaine 2.4, 2.31
"crack lung" 2.6
Crighton, D. 3.12
crime 2.15

dance drugs xiv
Darke, S. 3.17, 3.21
data collection xvii-xx, 4.1–50
  Communicable Disease Surveillance Centre 4.44–7
  coroners 5.10
  death certificates 5.15–19
  Department of the Environment, Transport and
  the Regions (DETR) 4.41–3
  drug type 6.10
  HBV 4.46–7
  HCV 4.46, 5.8–9
  improvements xx-xxii, xxxii, 5.1–27, 10.3, 10.5
  injection-transmitted virus diseases xxx-xxxii
  methadone 7.19

data collection—*contd*
  Northern Ireland 4.35
  St George's Hospital Medical School 4.38–40
  Scotland 4.31-4, 5.21
  toxicological examinations 5.11–14
  viral infections 5.7
data outputs xxii-xxiii
DATs *see* Drug Action Teams
death
  after release from prison 2.23
  causes of xix, xxi, 4.14, 4.24, 5.15
  delayed xii, 8.2
  mechanisms of 2.3
death certificates xviii, 4.16–19
  ONS 4.22
  recommendations xxi, 5.15–19
  social processes 3.2
decontamination procedures 9.18
definitions
  drug-related death 1.13
  immediate deaths 1.14
dehydration xiv, 2.33
delayed deaths xii, 8.2
delerium 2.31
delta virus 9.28
Department of the Environment, Transport and the
Regions (DETR) xx, 4.41–3
Department of Health, methadone prescriptions
xxv
dependence 2.20–1
depression
  suicide xvi, 2.15, 3.12–13, 8.32–4
  treatment 8.25
DETR *see* Department of the Environment,
Transport and the Regions
dextromoramide (Palfium) 2.27
DF118 2.27
diamorphine *see* heroin
diazepam (Valium) 2.36
Diconal xiv, 2.27
digestive disease, intravenous drug use 2.17
dihydrocodeine (DF118) 2.27
dipipanone with cyclizine (Diconal) 2.27
disinfection 9.36
disseminated intravascular coagulation 2.33
diversion xxviii
doctors *see* general practitioners
domestic violence 2.15
dopamine system 2.20
dose-dependency 2.4
driving
  see also road traffic accidents
  mental impairment xxix, 2.14
Drug Action Teams (DATs) xxxiv, 1.16, 10.19
  methadone deaths xxv, xxvi

Drug Arrest Referral Schemes xxix, 8.50
drug dealing, violence 2.15
drug interactions xii, 1.11, 2.42–5
  immediate death xv, xxvii
  methadone xxiv, 7.11
drugged driving xxix, 2.14
DVLA, notification 8.38

Ecstasy (MDMA)
  immediate death xiv, xxvii
  kidney damage 2.12
  liver damage 2.11
  pathology 2.9
  recommendations 8.19–20
education
  policy 8.10
  virus infections 9,32, 9,35, 9,39
EMCDDA *see* European Monitoring Centre for Drugs and Drug Addiction
emergency services xxviii-xxix, 8.40-9
employment 3.10
England and Wales
  data collection xviii-xix, xxii-xxiii, 4.8–30
  drug injection xxvi
  EMCDDA data xxii
  HCV 9.13
  methadone xxiv, 7.1
  social deprivation 3.10
  statistics 1.1
  trends 6.3–10, 6.14–15
  viral infection xxx-xxxi
Eskild, A. 2.24
European Monitoring Centre for Drugs and Drug Addiction (EMCDDA) xxii, 4.48–9, 6.1

families xxxiv, 10.18
Farrington, A. 3.7
fillers 2.19
forensic medical examiners xxix
friends, immediate deaths xxviii
Frischer, M. 3.7

gangrene 2.16
Garriet, J. 3.20
gender xvi, 3.6–7, 6.3
general practitioners (GPs)
  coroner notification 4.9–10
  interventions xxviii
General Register Office (GRO) (Scotland) xix
geographical location 6.6
Ghodse, A.H. 3.8, 3.10, 3.14, 3.15
Gossop, M. 2.24
GPs *see* general practitioners
GRO *see* General Register Office
Gutierrez-Cebollada, 3.15

Hall, W. 7.2
Hall, W.D. 2.18
Hammersley, R. 2.18, 2.42
HEA (England), drug injection xxvi
health authorities, methadone prescriptions xxv
heart 2.7–8
HEBS (Scotland), drug injection xxvi
hepatitis B virus (HBV) xiii, xx, xxx-xxxi, 9.1, 9.24–9
  data collection 4.46
  heroin 4.45
  viral carriage 9.6
hepatitis C virus (HCV)
  data collection 5.8–9
  deaths xiii, xx, 9.1, 9.13–23
  statistics xxx-xxxii, 1.4
  trends 9.4
  viral carriage 9.6
hepatitis D virus xxxi, 9.28
hepatitis G virus 9.7
heroin (diamorphine)
  availability 3.16
  deaths xxiii, 2.24–5, 6.10
  drug combinations 2.42
  HBV 4.45
  HCV status 9.14
  immediate deaths xxvi
  kidney damage 2.12
  methadone maintenance 7.10
  purity 2.18
  risk perception 3.17, 3.18
  Scotland xxiii
  suicide 2.4, 2.15
  tolerance xiv, 2.22
  withdrawal 2.21
HIV
  data collection xx, 4.44
  deaths xiii, xvi, xxx, 9.1, 9.8
  prison 3.13
  recommendations 9.9–12
  sociological research 3.2
  statistics 1.3
Home Office 4.37
homelessness 3.15
homicides 2.15, 8.57
Hope, V. *et al* 9.14
housing estates xxiii
Howard, D.J. 3.16
Hyatt, R.R. 3.16
hypertension 2.31
hyperthermia 2.8, 2.33
hyponatraemic collapse 2.34
hypothermia 2.8
hypoxia 2.29

ICD *see* International Classification of Diseases
immediate deaths
  definition 1.14, 2.1
  factors 2.4
  pathology and toxicology xii–xv, 2.1–46
  recommendations xii, xxvi–xxix, 8.7
income 3.11
infection
  injected drugs 9.30
  intravenous drug use 2.17
infective endocarditis 2.13
injected drugs xiii, 2.4, 2.16
  agency policy xxxii
  HCV 9.17–19
  immediate death xxvi
  infection 9.30
  recommendations 8.9–10, 10.10
  risk xiv, 2.17
  statistics 1.4
  viral infections xxx–xxxii, 2.13
inquests xviii, xxi, 4.9, 4.14, 10.18
interferon xxxi, 9.22, 9.29
International Classification of Diseases (ICD) xix, 4.23–6, 6.1, 6.2
  recommendations xxii
interventions, general practitioners (GPs) xxviii
intranasal administration 2.4, 2.16
intravenous administration *see* injected drugs

kidney damage xiii, 2.12

LAAM *see* levo-alpha-acetyl methadol
levo-alpha-acetyl methadol (LAAM) 7.21
liver cancer xxxi, 1.4, 9.21
liver damage xiii, 2.11
location 3.14
LSD *see* lysergic acid diethylamide
lungs 2.5–6, 2.25
lysergic acid diethylamide (LSD) xv, 2.40

mandatory testing 5.13
Manning, F. 3.20
manufacturing errors 2.4
marker detection 9.5
Martindale 7.4
MDMA *see* Ecstasy
men xvi, xxiii, 3.6–7
mental function, impairment 2.14
mental health xvi, xxviii, 8.30
mental health status 3.12–13
methadone xiv, xxiv–xxvi, xxxiii, 7.1–22, 8.5
  alternatives 7.21
  death by 2.26
  guidelines 7.16
  immediate deaths xxvi

methadone—*contd*
  prisoners xxix
  Scotland xxiii
  tolerance 2.4
3,4-methylenedioxymethamphetamine *see* MDMA
Misuse of Drugs Act (1971) xi, 8.37
Misuse of Drugs (Notification of and Supply to Addicts) Regulations (1973) 4.37
misuse prevention 1.8
modality 2.16–17
mood swings 2.4, 2.15
morphine
  see also heroin
  tolerance 2.22
motor vehicle accidents xii, 1.3
myocardial infarction 2.7, 2.29

Nakamura, G. 3.20
naloxone xxviii, xxix, 8.28, 8.45–9
national surveys, virus status xx
needle exchanges 9.32, 9.37
Nothern Ireland xii
  data collection xix, xxii, 4.35
  statistics 1.2
  trends 6.13

O'Doherty, M. 3.7
Office of National Statistics (ONS) xix, xxii, 4.22–30
  data base improvements 5.3, 5.22–4
  restricted approach xxii
  standard approach xxii–xxiii
ONS *see* Office of National Statistics
opiate-induced asthma 2.6
opioids xiv, 2.27, 8.4, 8.6
  Australia 1.6
  methadone treatment xxiv
  toxicology 2.5
  withdrawl 2.21
Oppenheimer, E. 2.24, 3.7, 3.8
oral administration 2.4, 2.16
overdose xiv
  see also tolerance
  cocaine 2.31
  death certificates 4.18
  drug agency premises xxviii
  emergency services xxviii
  heroin 2.24
  intravenous drug use 2.17
  public awareness xxxiii
  risk perception 3.20–1
  statistics 1.1
  witnesses 8.42–3

Palfium 2.27

pathology
  see also toxicology
  immediate deaths 2.1–46
  reports xviii, 4.14
personal factors xvi–xvii
pharmacists 8.37
pharmacology 2.3
poisoning xviii
police
  arestees 8.50–1
  Drug Arrest Referral Scheme xxix, 8.50
  reports xviii
police stations, naloxone 8.46
police surgeons xxix, 8.50
policy
  see also recommendations
  data base improvements 5.2
  education 8.10
  framework xxxii–xxxiv, 10.1–22
  methadone 7.14–16
  misuse prevention 1.8
  national 5.23
  risk assessment 8.23–4
post mortems
  coroner's order xviii, 4.12
  toxicological examinations 4.12, 4.20, 5.11–14
Pottieger, A.E. 2.32
prescriptions
  benzodiazepines xxvii
  controlled drugs xxvii
  diversion of 8.29
  methadone xxiv, xxv, 7.17
  recommendations 8.11–13, 10.3, 10.11
prevalence xvii
Prevention Working Group (PWG) xi
price xvi, 3.16
primary care xxviii, 8.35–8
prisons
  fatalities after release 2.23
  naloxone 8.46
  recommendations xxix, xxxiii, 10.3, 10.12
  Scotland 8.58
  suicide 3.12
  virus infections xxxii, 9.34–8
procurators fiscal xix–xx, xxii, 4.31, 5.21
protease inhibitors 9.12
public awareness xxxiii, 10.3, 10.6, 10.7
public places xv, 3.15
pulmonary embolism 2.16
pulmonary eodema 2.25
purity xiv, 2.4, 2.18
PWG see Prevention Working Group

readership 1.16
recommendations 8.3, 10.1

recommendations—contd
  alcohol 8.7
  benzodiazepines 8.7, 8.14–16
  causes of death 4.24
  cocaine 8.7
  Ecstasy 8.19–20
  HIV 9.9–12
  immediate deaths xii, xxvi–xxix, 8.7
  injected drugs 8.9–10, 10.10
  mental health 8.30–4
  prescriptions 8.11–12, 10.3, 10.12
  primary care 8.35–8
  prisons xxix, xxxiii, 9.34–8, 10.3, 10.12
  road traffic accidents 8.56
  training 10.3, 10.14
  treatment agencies 10.3, 10.8, 10.9, 10.10, 10.13
  virus infections 9.2, 9.31–3
  VSA 8.17–18
Registrar of Births Deaths and Marriages xviii, 4.9, 4.21
relatedness xvii–xviii
relatives, immediate deaths xxviii
research xxxiv
residential areas xxiii
residential treatment, loss of tolerance 2.23
respiration xiii, 2.5–6, 2.8
respiratory depression xv, 2.24, 2.25
respiratory disease, intravenous drug use 2.17
resuscitation techniques xxviii, 8.28
rhabdomyolysis 2.12
Rhodes, T. 3.16, 3.18, 3.19
ribavirin xxxi, 9.22
risk xiv
  assessment 8.23–4, 8,27
  behaviour xvi, xxviii, 2.14
  factors 2.16–23
  methadone maintenance 7.9, 7.13
  overdose xvi–xvii
  perception 3.17–21
  public places 3.15
road traffic accidents xii, 1.3
  alcohol 2.38
  cannabis xiv, 2.28
  data collection xviii, xx, xxii, 4.41–3, 5.25
  drugged driving xxix
  mental impairment 2.14
  recommendations 8.56
Roberts, I. et al 2.24
Ross, J. 3.17, 3.21

St George's Hospital Medical School xix–xx, 4.38–40
Scotland xii
  AIDS xxx, 9.8
  benzodiazepines xxiii

Scotland—*contd*
  data collection xix, xxii, 4.31–4, 5.21
  drug injection xxvi
  HCV 9.13
  heroin xxiii
  ICD10 4.30
  methadone xxiii, xxv, 7.1, 7.20
  overdose 8.8
  prison policy 8.58
  social deprivation 3.10
  statistics 1.2
  trends xxiii, 6.11–12
screening, virus infections 9.32
Seaman, S.R. 2.23
sedatives 2.35
selective serotonin reuptake inhibitors (SSRIs) 8.25, 8.34
septicaemia xiii, xxxi, 9.30
  intravenous drug use 2.13
Shewan, D. 2.23
situational factors xvi–xvii
sleeping pills 2.35
smoking xii, 1.11
  administration route 2.16
snorting, administration route 2.16
social class 3.10–1
social deprivation xvi, xxiii, xxxiii, 3.10, 6.7–9, 6.15
  recommendations 10.3, 10.15
    VSA 1.10
social factors xvi–xvii, 3.1
sociological research 3.2–5
SSRIs *see* selective serotonin reuptake inhibitors
sterile water xxxii, 9,32
strokes xiii, 2.9–10
Sturner, W. 3.20
sudden death *see* immediate death
suicide xiv, 2.4, 2.15, 3.2, 8.31–4
  cannabis 2.28
  mental health xvi, 3.12–13
  primary care 8.35
  prison 3.12
  withdrawl symptoms 8.54
sweating 2.8

tablets 8.13
Tardiff, K. 2.32
Taylor, M. 2.24
Temazepam 2.36
Temgesic 2.27
thrombosis 2.16
tolerance
  death after release 8.55
  immediate death xxvi, 2.4
  loss of 2.23, 8.8
  methadone 7.7

toothbrushes 9.19
Towl, G. 3.12
toxicity
  amphetamine sulphate 2.39
  cannabis 2.28
  cocaine 2.29
  immediate deaths xiii, 2.3
  modality 2.16–17
toxicological examinations xviii, xxi, 4.12, 4.20, 5.11–14
toxicology
  see also pathology
  immediate deaths 2.1–46
  lungs 2.5–6
training
  A&E departments 8.39, 8.44
  coroners xxi, 5.20
  doctors 4.10
  immediate deaths policies xxvii
  methadone prescriptions xxv
  policy xxxiii
  recommendations 10.3, 10.14
  treatment agencies 8.26
  virus infections xxxi–xxxii, 9.32–3
transfusion transmitted virus (TTV) 9.7
trauma, intravenous drug use 2.17
treatment agencies
  action plan 8.25
  immediate deaths policies xxvii
  injected drugs xxvi
  injected drugs policies xxxiii
  overdoses 8.42
  prison links 8.53
  recommendations 10.3, 10.8, 10.9, 10.10, 10.13
  responsibilites xxvii–xxviii
  resuscitation techniques xxviii, 8.28
  risk assessment 8.27
  virus infections 9.31–3
  virus status surveys xx
trends 4.3, 6.1–16
  virus infections 9.3, 9.4
TTV *see* transfusion transmitted virus

unemployment xvi
user characteristics 3.6–23
user responsibilities xxxiii

vaccines
  HBV xxxi, 9.26, 9.38
  HCV 9.16
Valium 2.36
vasodilation 2.8
violence xii, xiv
  alcohol 2.38
  mental impairment 2.14–15

violence disease, intravenous drug use 2.17
viral carriage 9.5
viral status
  national surveys xx
  suicide 3.22
virus infections
  data collection xx, 5.7
  deaths xii, xiii, xxvi, xxx–xxxii, 1.3, 2.13
  primary care 8.35
  prisons 9.34–8
  public awareness xxxiii
  recommendations 9.2, 9.31–3
  treatment agencies 9.31–3
  trends 9.3, 9.4
volatile substance abuse (VSA) xii, xv, 1.10, 2.41, 8.7
  data collection xvii, 4.6
  ICD9 4.26
  immediate death xxvi, xxvii
  recommendations 8.17–18
  social deprivation 3.10
  young people 3.8

volatile substance abuse (VSA)—contd
vomit, aspiration of 2.25, 2.38
VSA see volatile substance abuse

Walsh, R. 3.20
water intoxication xiv, 2.4, 2.34
Williams, A.G. et al 2.28
withdrawl 2.20–1
  suicide 8.54
women xvi, xxiii, 3.6–7
World Health Organisation 9.27

years of life lost 6.5, 8.6
young people
  accidental deaths 2.24
  immediate death xxvi
  Scotland 4.32
  VSA 3.8

Zador, D. et al 3.20